THE

BRECON & ABERGAVENNY

SECTION OF THE MONMOUTHSHIRE & BRECON

CANAL

John Norris

AUTHOR'S NOTE

My wife and I first cruised the 'Mon & Brec' in 1975. We returned with increasing frequency and affection until in 1988 we decided on a boat of our own. Archimedes was launched in 1989 and apart from a year spent continuously cruising on the main system in 1996/97 we have been here ever since, held in thrall by the magic of this matchless canal and its surroundings.

In the first edition of the guide, published in 1991, I expressed the hope that it would help others to gain something of the enjoyment that we had ourselves experienced. From the many kind comments that I have received it is clear that I have not been disappointed. I hope that this fourth edition will be found no less useful than its predecessors.

It is interesting to reflect briefly on the changes that have occurred along the canal during the twelve years since the first edition. It is sad that, as elsewhere, a number of village shops and post offices along the canal have closed, a loss both to the local community and to visitors. However, the pubs are flourishing! On the positive side the canal is undoubtedly in better shape. British Waterways have maintained and improved its condition and added greatly to its facilities. The current major dredging programme has already much improved cruising conditions 'down the bottom end'. British Waterways are active participants, with local authorities and other bodies, in the Regeneration Partnership which is working towards the restoration of the Monmouthshire section. Restoration of navigation to Newport is no longer a question of 'if' but 'when'.

Meanwhile, the Monmouthshire is well worth following on foot and I have extended the Appendix to include basic maps covering the entire surviving line, with a brief commentary. I have also introduced an element of colour into the maps on the continuously navigable section of the joint canal.

As with previous editions I am indebted to all those who have so kindly helped with advice and information. I must mention with particular gratitude Ray Haydon, archivist of the Monmouthshire, Brecon and Abergavenny Canals Trust, who has furnished me with information and guided my hand on the Monmouthshire details.

John Norris   July 2003

CONTENTS

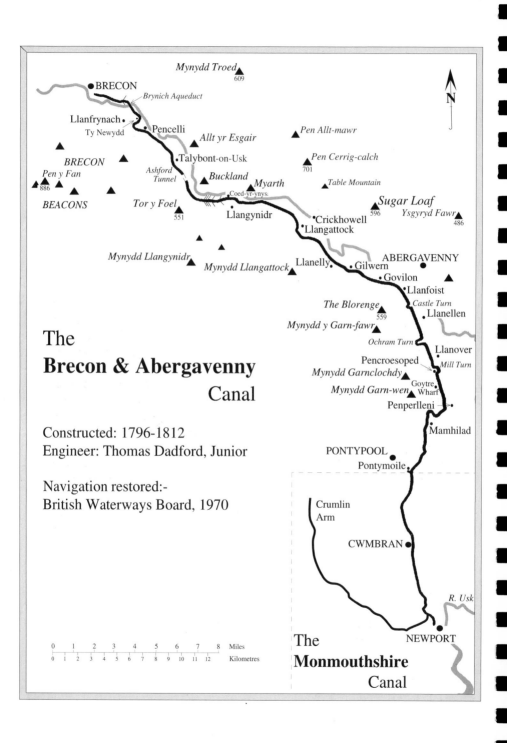

The
Brecon & Abergavenny
Canal

Constructed: 1796-1812
Engineer: Thomas Dadford, Junior

Navigation restored:-
British Waterways Board, 1970

The
Monmouthshire
Canal

Mynydd Troed▲
609

●BRECON

Brynich Aqueduct

Llanfrynach●
Ty Newydd   ●Pencelli

Allt yr Esgair▲

●*Pen Allt-mawr*

▲

Pen Cerrig-calch▲
701

BRECON   ▲   ●Talybont-on-Usk
Pen y Fan   *Ashford*   *Buckland*
▲   *Tunnel*   *Myarth*   *Table Mountain*
886 ▲ ▲   ▲   Coed-yr-ynys.

Sugar Loaf
BEACONS   *Tor y Foel*   596   *Ysgyryd Fawr*▲
551   Llangynidr   ●Crickhowell   486
●Llangattock

▲

Mynydd Llangynidr▲   Lanelly● ●Gilwern   **ABERGAVENNY** ●
Mynydd Llangattock▲   ●Govilon
▲   ●Llanfoist

The Blorenge▲   *Castle Turn*
559   ●Llanellen
Mynydd y Garn-fawr▲

Ochram Turn   Llanover●
Pencroesoped   *Mill Turn*
Mynydd Garnclochdy▲   Goytre
Mynydd Garn-wen▲ *Wharf*
Penperlleni

●Mamhilad

PONTYPOOL
●   Pontymoile●

Crumlin
Arm

CWMBRAN ●

R. Usk

NEWPORT

| 0 | 1 | 2 | 3 | 4 | 5 | 6 | 7 | 8 | Miles |
| 0 | 1 2 | 3 | 4 | 5 6 | 7 | 8 9 | 10 | 11 12 | Kilometres |

INTRODUCTION

The Brecon and Abergavenny Canal is a gem among canals. Set in some of the most beautiful scenery in Britain and lying almost wholly within or along the border of the Brecon Beacons National Park, the canal hugs the mountainside above the valley of the River Usk for much of the 33 miles between its terminus at Brecon and its junction with the Monmouthshire Canal at Pontymoile. For 23 of those miles, the canal remains on one level, a fine piece of contour-following in hilly terrain, and one of the longest lock-free pounds in the inland waterway system.

There are superb views across field and valley to other mountains, far and near. With every twist and turn the scene changes – wooded banks and cuttings give way to open views and valleys to mountain peaks. The mountain that a moment ago appeared to be slipping behind is suddenly in front again. Almost throughout, the rural character remains. Though never far from civilisation, there is an abundance of wild life and the canal is beautiful in all seasons, whether in winter's frost, springtime's blossom, summer's leaf or autumn's fall.

Yet despite its tranquil nature and idyllic setting, the Brecon & Abergavenny is in every sense a 'real' canal, with a tunnel, locks, a fine aqueduct, attractive bridges, and relics of the past for those who care to look for them. What is now so quiet and peaceful was once a very artery of South Wales, carrying not only agricultural produce from farm to market but linking with nearly two hundred miles of horse-drawn tramroad to convey coal, limestone, iron ore and iron from colliery and quarry to town and kiln, furnace and forge; coal for houses, for iron smelting and lime burning; limestone for fluxing iron in the furnace and for burning in canalside kilns to produce lime for agriculture and building; iron ore for the iron to feed the industrial revolution and provide the rails for the transport system that would one day devour the canals.

In its heyday, in the 1820s, the canal carried over 30,000 tons of coal and coke, 30,000 tons of iron and 12,000 tons of lime and limestone a year. At Gilwern and Govilon, at Llanfoist and Talybont, at Llangattock and Brecon the now silent wharves once rang with the squealing of tram wheels, the noise of horses and the sounds of men at work.

5

INDUSTRIAL HISTORY

 It is usually said, based on words in Walter Davies' *General View of the Agriculture and Domestic Economy of South Wales*, 1814, that the Brecknock & Abergavenny Canal originated with a group of local Breconshire and Monmouthshire people with the intention (and result) of facilitating and cheapening the transport of coal, lime and agricultural produce.

However, it seems likely that there was more to it than this. As well as the many local people, great and small, among the shareholders there were ironmasters too and it can hardly be coincidence that the ancient symbol for iron ♂ was included on the Canal Company seal – the iron trade must have been in the minds of some right from the start.

Among the larger shareholders was Samuel Homfray, who later described himself as the 'Father of the Canal'. Also there was the Duke of Beaufort, who was well served by the Brecon & Abergavenny and Monmouthshire canals and their associated tramroads. His royalties on coal, iron ore and limestone extracted from his mountain land in the parishes of Llangattock and Llanelly (Gilwern) increased thirty fold in twenty years.

The Act of Parliament authorising the promoters to construct the canal and associated tramroads was passed in March 1793. Initially the intention was that the canal would run from Brecon to a junction with the River Usk north of Newport. However the Monmouthshire Canal Company, whose canal was to run from Newport to Pontnewynydd, north-west of Pontypool, with a branch from Malpas up the Ebbw valley to Crumlin, saw mutual advantages in the Brecon & Abergavenny Canal terminating in a junction with its canal at Pontymoile instead of joining the Usk. The Monmouthshire Company not only offered water but also provided £3000 towards the cost of the new canal and agreed that its toll rates for goods travelling to and from the Brecon & Abergavenny would be no higher than the Brecon & Abergavenny's own rates. The toll agreement was enshrined in the Act of Parliament authorising the Brecon & Abergavenny canal; it later proved to be something of a two-edged sword to the Monmouthshire Company.

The canal company's first work was the construction of a railroad (i.e. a horse-drawn tram way using edge rails rather than flanged tram plates) to bring coal down from collieries at Gellifelen to Llangrwyney Forge and to the Abergavenny-Brecon turnpike road by Llangrwney (and later the canal at Gilwern) to supply the 'country at large'. Pig iron for the forge also came down the railroad, which opened in 1794. John Dadford was the Engineer.

The Engineer for the canal was Thomas Dadford Junr., John's brother. Thomas was engineer also of the Monmouthshire canal and, with his brothers James and John and their father, Thomas, was involved in the construction of many of the canals in South Wales. The design of the canal was neither 'broad' nor 'narrow' but 'narrowish', with locks designed to take boats approximately 63 ft. long and 9 ft. wide, similar to the Dadfords' other Welsh canals. Thomas Dadford Senr. had worked on James Brindley's Staffordshire and Worcestershire Canal and photographs of the rather crude South Wales boats, with their exposed knees, seem very reminiscent of Brindley's earlier 'starvationers'.

Cutting of the canal started at Penpedairheol, two miles to the west of Gilwern, in April 1796. Construction of the great embankment across the River Clydach, including the aqueduct bridge for the river and the tunnel for the railroad, commenced a year later. The first section of canal, from Gilwern to Llangynidr, was opened late in 1797. Extension westwards was completed to Talybont late in 1799 and to Brecon in December 1800. Cutting was let in lots. Amongst the numerous contractors were Jonathan Gee of Neath, Thomas Greatrex of Crickhowell (farmer), William Macdonald of Matlock, Edward Price of Llangynidr, Thomas Powell of Abergavenny, William Parry of Tretower (gent), Thomas Parry of Llangattock (shopkeeper), Thomas and Evan Lloyd of Llanelly (Gilwern) and William Watkins of Llanvihangel Talyllyn. Benjamin James was the mason for the bridges, aqueducts, culverts, locks and tunnel.

Trade on the canal was soon established by the Brecknock Boat Co., carrying principally coal and limestone. The company prospered and its fleet of wooden boats, each able to carry up to about 24 tons and drawing 3 ft. when fully loaded, increased from five in 1798 to twenty in 1806.

Extension of the canal eastwards resumed late in 1802 and was completed to Govilon in January 1805. The Engineer & Contractor for this length was Thomas Cartwright (Thomas Dadford Junr. having died in 1801).

There was then a lull. The fund-raising powers of the Act of 1793 had been exhausted and a supplementary Act passed in 1804 had proved disappointing. Pressure from the Monmouthshire Canal Company and the need for transport facilities for the growing iron industry provided the spur, and a loan of £30,000 from ironmaster Richard Crawshay the means, to resume construction in 1809. The link with the Monmouthshire Canal at Pontymoile was finally achieved in February 1812. William Crosley was the Engineer for the section from Govilon to Pontymoile. The contractors were Thomas Dunn, Peter Murphy and William Seed.

A long period of competition between the two canals followed.

Ironmasters seeking transport for their products to Newport and the sea and already connected to the Monmouthshire canal by tramroad saw the advantage of laying alternative tramroads to the Brecon & Abergavenny to take advantage of its lower toll rates, which the Monmouthshire Company then had to accept, in accordance with the provisions of the 1793 Act for goods travelling through.

At first there was business and profit for both canals and when hard times came the causes were largely external. The growing railway system, which had provided much of the demand for the iron, the carriage of which had helped to make the canals so profitable, now offered cheaper transport. Better quality imported iron ores began to replace the indigenous resources of the region. Steel making began to supersede iron. By the 1860s the iron and coal trade had gone from the canals as large railway-connected steelworks using imported ore replaced small canal-connected ironworks.

In 1865 the Brecon & Abergavenny Canal was bought by the Monmouthshire Company. The latter, hampered by the conversion of the Pontnewynydd arm of their canal into a railway in 1853, were now largely dependent on the B&A's flow of water from the Usk at Brecon, not least for the continued sale of water to Newport Docks.

In 1880 the joint concern was taken over by the Great Western Railway. Renumbering of bridges and locks, the addition of weight restriction notices and the erection of GWR boundary posts followed the takeover, as did the use of the title Monmouthshire and Brecon for the joint canal.

By the 1920s commercial trade had fallen almost to nothing. The last toll on the B&A section (a 1-ton cargo of lime from Llangynidr to Govilon) was taken at Llangynidr on 22 February 1933. The Monmouthshire was largely abandoned but the Brecon & Abergavenny survived as a water feeder, albeit in a state of some neglect. In 1952 its fortunes began to turn. An effective campaign and rally organised by the Inland Waterways Association raised public interest and plans to culvert a number of bridges were abandoned. Pleasure boating was active by the early 1960s and in 1968 British Waterways commenced restoration. In 1970, with restoration of the drawbridge at Talybont, the Brecon & Abergavenny was reopened from end to end, surviving those very railways which had helped to destroy its commercial viability! The cost of restoration was jointly borne by Monmouthshire and Breconshire County Councils through the Brecon Beacons National Park Committee. The current use of the title Monmouthshire and Brecon fittingly reflects their farsighted action.

In its present form, the continuously navigable section of the 'Mon & Brec' comprises the entire length of the Brecon & Abergavenny Canal, save for the final lost 200 yards at Brecon, plus a short length of the Monmouth-shire Canal, from Pontymoile to Five Locks, Cwmbran. Crown Bridge at Sebastopol, culverted in the 1950s, was reconstructed by Torfaen Borough Council in 1994, assisted by grants from the EEC, the Welsh Development Agency and Gwent C.C. The section from Crown Bridge to Five Locks was restored and a new basin constructed in 1996. It was officially opened by the Mayor of Torfaen on 24 May 1997. Eventual restoration to Newport no longer seems a pipedream. Meanwhile, much of the main line and Crumlin arm of the Monmouthshire remains 'in water'. The towpath is available for walking and exploration is recommended

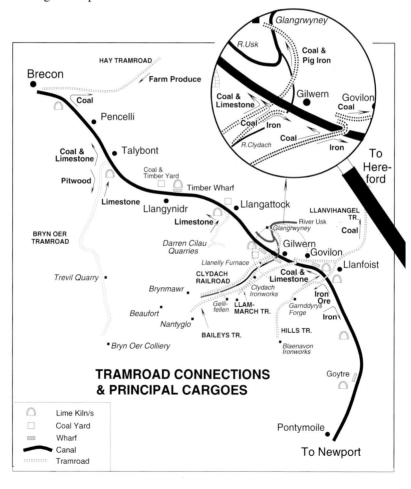

TRAMROAD CONNECTIONS & PRINCIPAL CARGOES

9

NATURAL HISTORY

The canal constitutes a fine nature trail, for within its 33 mile length is a wide and interesting diversity of trees, plants and other wildlife.

For much of its length the canal is tree lined, not only by the ubiquitous alder but also by a variety of other species including oak, ash, sycamore, willow, sweet chestnut and hawthorn. There are fine beeches in many parts, most notably on the hillside above Llanfoist, stretching through nearly to Govilon.

In spring, primroses, bluebells, violets and celandines are amongst the wild flowers decorating the canal banks. The blossom of wild cherries between Crickhowell and Llangynidr, and elsewhere towards Brecon, is followed as the year advances by rhododendrons at Llangattock and buddleia at many points. Reed mace and yellow flag are amongst the plants gracing the water's edge in summer, complemented by rosebay willowherb and foxgloves at the back of the towpath and elsewhere. Arrowhead, with its distinctive arrow-shaped leaves, is common in the lower reaches towards Pontymoile.

As summer moves towards autumn the brilliant red and orange berries of the rowan add their colourful contribution. Wild raspberries, elderberries and an abundance of blackberries offer themselves within (fairly) easy reach. Hazel nuts follow and one can join the grey squirrels in the queue – shells opened by them can often be found on the towpath. In autumn, the beeches in particular are beautiful in their glowing colours, while the varied species on Myarth hill provide a feast of variegated colour on the far side of the river.

Ducks and their broods are a common sight in spring and early summer. Mallards there are aplenty, despite the growing number of ducks of 'indeterminate origin'. Moorhens can also be seen. Swans visit the canal intermittently and a pair raised a brood of seven cygnets in 2001. Water voles are now a rarity. The occasional mink, black and large stoat-sized, is a poor substitute for the vole. Originally escapees from fur farms, the mink are voracious and unwelcome predators.

Pondskaters, a little like daddy longlegs in appearance, rush about on the surface of the water, particularly in the upper reaches nearer Brecon. Above the water blue damsel flies abound in summer while beneath the surface a variety of coarse fish, roach, dace, perch, bream, gudgeon, and mirror carp among them, await or evade the angler. In the clearer waters near Brecon eels and even grass snakes may be seen swimming in the canal. Frogs and toads are common, though more often heard than seen.

The trees and shrubs provide habitat for a wide variety of common garden and woodland birds, among them tits, woodpeckers, nuthatches and treecreepers. Wrens are common. In winter, migrant siskins can be seen feeding on the seeds in the alder cones. In spring the liquid song of the curlew may be heard in wet meadowland and in summer it is a delight to watch swallows swooping low over the water for insects or dipping in for refreshment. Buzzards, once a rarity, are now common, particularly over the section from Llangynidr towards Brecon. The mewing of the buzzard by day is as distinctive a sound as the hooting of the tawny owl by night. A solitary red kite (distinguishable from the buzzard by its forked tail) has been seen at the Brecon end of the canal and hopefully it will not be too long before kites have returned to the area around the canal. The grey wagtail, with its blue-grey head and back and vivid yellow underparts, may be seen at Brynich, where the canal crosses the river. So too may the dipper.

However, the two birds which best represent the canal are the heron and the kingfisher. Herons may be encountered irregularly almost anywhere along the canal but one spot where a lone heron is often to be seen is near Birdspool Bridge below Goytre. While herons have increased in number, there seems to have been a reduction in kingfisher numbers in recent years.

You are unlikely to miss the heron's dramatic departure as it takes off in front of you, even if you fail to notice its motionless presence at the water's edge until it moves. The diminutive kingfisher (much smaller than you may imagine if you have not seen one before) is much easier to miss but once seen is not forgotten. As you approach its quiet perch, often on a low overhanging branch, the kingfisher will fly ahead, speeding low across the water and rising to a new perch at the side of the canal. If the light and angle are right you may be rewarded with the brilliant blue flash of its back or orange of its underparts and hear its distinctive call – a short repeated whistle. If you are lucky you may witness the performance several times as the kingfisher moves ahead at your approach until at the end of its territory it leaves the canal to fly back behind you.

To see a kingfisher take a fish or find one on your mooring rope in the morning is a rare treat.

GENERAL INFORMATION

PLANNING YOUR CRUISE

Although the canal is only 33 miles long from Pontymoile to Brecon, a return cruise will easily fill a week, particularly if you take time off to explore some of the attractions en route.

If you like to keep in touch with civilisation you may well prefer, at least initially, the 22 mile section between Llanfoist and Brecon. The canal passes through villages at intervals and the B4558 is often close at hand or actually adjacent to the canal.

If you like isolation you may prefer the section below Llanfoist. Here the feel of the canal is different. Although civilisation is never far away, the canal passes through no villages. At the lower end its mountainside position is not matched by hills rising on the other side of the Usk valley and there is a sense of remoteness and tranquillity quite different from the canal above Llanfoist. It is none the less attractive for that.

Many hirers travel only as far south as Goytre Wharf. This is a pity. There are attractive features below Goytre and if time permits it is well worth while completing the journey to Pontymoile and beyond into the restored section of the Monmouthshire Canal. Recent major dredging works have brought this section up to the standard of the rest of the canal.

ADVANCE PREPARATION

The Bibliography near the end of this guide lists books and useful leaflets. Most of the items are readily available from bookshops and tourist information centres in the area. The B.W. Information, Heritage, Activity and Study Centre at Goytre Wharf stocks a large range of canal-related material.

SPEED

The canal is shallow and the British Waterways requirement not to make a breaking wash will severely limit your speed. You will certainly not be able to approach the 4 mph maximum speed limit. (Lest there be any doubt, if the rise and fall of water along the edge of the canal bank as you pass along is topped by a white-crested breaking wave running with the boat, you are making a wash and damaging the bank!). Apart from the concrete lined sections, it is rarely possible to exceed about 2½ miles an hour without creating a wash. Extra power is counter-productive, serving to do little more than damage the banks and drag the stern ever nearer the bottom of the canal. For planning purposes, it is sensible to allow no more than 2 mph.

If planning a cruise in detail, it is common to reckon a lock as equivalent in time to one mile, dividing distance in 'lock-miles' by average speed to give journey time. With practice, a lock on the Brecon & Abergavenny may take less than half as long as a mile of cruising but allowing time to take care is important and you may in any case have to wait for other boats at the lock/s before you.

A table of bridges and distances is included near the end of the guide.

MOORINGS

It is generally permissible to moor against the towpath wherever you can do so without obstructing the passage of other boats. Apart, therefore, from locks, bridgeholes, bends, winding holes, blind spots and narrow sections, mooring is almost unrestricted. In practice broken and shallow edges sometimes make it difficult to moor within plank distance of the bank and it is not always possible to stop exactly where one wishes. There are also lengths of experimental bank protection at and near Talybont using loose rocks, where mooring is neither permitted nor practicable. Remember that mooring lines must not cross the towpath.

There are mooring bollards or rings at Gilwern, Llangynidr, Talybont, Pencelli (Royal Oak), Brynich and Brecon. A number of other mooring spots favoured by the author are included on the strip maps. These include moorings within two hours cruising of the various hire bases on the canal.

MILEPOSTS AND BRIDGE NUMBERS

Mileposts were erected at ¼ mile intervals. The present positions date from after the amalgamation of the Brecon & Abergavenny with the Monmouthshire in 1865 and show distances from Llanarth Street, Newport, the shortened end of navigation in use between 1879 and 1930. Generally, only posts at whole miles showed the mileage total, the quarter mile posts giving just the fraction. Remains of nearly twenty stumps survive. Sadly, almost all the surviving intact posts were stolen in 1992/3; the remainder being then removed by BW for safekeeping. The 9 mile post, removed previously to the Valley Inheritance Museum, was situated about 60 yards north of Pontymoile junction. Deducting 9 miles from the mileages indicated by the posts therefore gives the approx. distance from Pontymoile.

Bridges were numbered from a similar point but the sequence also included bridges on the Crumlin branch of the Monmouthshire. Those on the Brecon & Abergavenny thus run from 52 at Pontymoile to 167 at Brecon. The locks are numbered according to the same philosophy, those on the Brecon & Abergavenny being numbered from 64 to 69. Bridges not the responsibility of the canal company were until recently unnumbered but have now been given 'A' numbers.

NAVIGATING THROUGH BRIDGEHOLES

All bridges require care, for the safety of both boat and crew. Bridges are generally low and sitting or lying on the roof when on the move is not recommended. Damage to cabin corners is most likely to occur at arched bridges on right hand bends when travelling upstream, i.e. towards Brecon. Drawbridges also pose a hazard, as the deck only opens to about 45°.

At arched bridges, aim to keep close to the towpath edge to gain maximum headroom. At Talybont electric drawbridge keep close to the open side.

The following bridges require particular care (not always obvious in advance):- 81, Tod's (between 95 & 96), 100, Heads of the Valleys (betw. 101 & 102), 103, 121, 134, 147, 156. Further details of these and other awkward bridges are given in the commentary accompanying the strip maps.

SOUND SIGNALS

The Rule of the Road is to keep to the right when passing an oncoming boat and to overtake on the left, as if driving a car on the Continent. There is a useful, if little used, code of sound signals recommended by British Waterways for indicating intentions when changing course. Derived from the International Regulations for Preventing Collisions at Sea but expressed in distinctly non-nautical language, the most useful signals are:-
1 short blast – I'm turning to the right
2 short blasts – I'm turning to the left
3 short blasts – I'm in reverse
One long blast every twenty seconds when approaching blind spots.

BUS SERVICES

Bus services run between Abergavenny and Brecon and between Newport and Abergavenny, connecting villages en route. The services can be reached from various points along the canal. For details contact Stagecoach Red and White [Tel. 0870 6082608]. For groups of three or more a taxi may be cheaper.

FISHING PERMITS

A permit and (for those over 12 years of age) a rod licence are required for fishing (including from a boat). Much of the canal is licensed to local angling clubs and day permits may be obtained from patrolling bailiffs. Further details and permits for unlicensed stretches may be obtained from the B.W. information centre at Goytre Wharf.

CYCLING

The towpath from Brecon to Brynich has been widened and surfaced to allow cycling. The work to create the 'Brynich Cycleway' was partly funded by the European Agricultural Guidance and Guarantee Fund.

MONMOUTHSHIRE, BRECON & ABERGAVENNY CANALS TRUST

The Trust was formed in 1984 to promote the joint canal and in particular the regeneration of the Monmouthshire section south of Pontymoile. Further information may be obtained from the registered office at 95 The Highway, New Inn, Pontypool, Torfaen NP4 0PN or from the Trust's web site at http://www.mon-brec-canal-trust.org.uk

GENERAL HINTS (Guiding principles, not inviolable rules)

Propeller damage is expensive and holiday consuming so:-
    When leaving a mooring push the boat out before engaging the propeller
    If appropriate reverse out into deeper water before going forward.
    In the shallows, use the pole in preference to the engine.
When aground, try reversing off – the way in is usually the best way out!
Use poles from boat to bank, not vice-versa – ends can easily slip!
Don't dangle arms and legs over the side of the boat and don't use them to fend off boats or bridges – boats survive impact much better than limbs!
When approaching the bank to moor, avoid hauling on the bow rope lest the stern should swing out. If it does, and a stern rope has not been taken, pointing the tiller towards the bank and giving a brief burst of forward throttle while the stern is still in deep water will bring it round.
ONE DEFINITE RULE:- If you raise the weed hatch to clear the propeller, don't forget to stop the engine first and replace the cover securely before restarting. (A short burst in reverse will sometimes clear suspected fouling, including weed and autumn leaves, without the need to raise the hatch.)

ACCIDENT AND EMERGENCY DEPARTMENTS

    The Royal Gwent Hospital, Cardiff Road, Newport
    Nevill Hall Hospital, Brecon Road, Abergavenny.
There is a minor casualty department at:-
    Brecon War Memorial Hospital, Cerrigcochion Road, Brecon.

OPERATING THE LOCKS ON THE B&A

The following information and advice is offered in good faith as an 'aide memoire' but is not intended as a substitute for proper instruction. No responsibility can be accepted by the author and publisher for any accidents arising from incorrect operation of the locks. Hirers unfamiliar with the locks on this canal must ensure that they are properly briefed by their hire company. *The Boaters Handbook*, published by British Waterways, gives comprehensive information on lock operation as well as on other aspects of boating and related safety procedures. The Code is available free of charge from Customer Services, British Waterways, Willow Grange, Church Road, Watford, Herts WD1 3QA. A small quantity is held at the BW Information, Heritage, Activity and Study Centre at Goytre wharf.

Locks are the 'steps' by which a canal ascends or descends the countryside and no canal holiday would be fully complete without them. They are simple to operate if you take your time and work through step by step. It is, however, all too easy to become overawed by the prospect and to allow rational thought to give way to irregular action. A little advance thought and planning will help to keep 'brain in gear' when the time comes.

The principle of operation is straightforward. To travel 'uphill' a boat enters an empty lock from the lower level, the bottom gates are closed, the lock is filled, the top gate is opened and the boat leaves. Travelling 'downhill' the process is reversed; the boat enters a full lock at high level, the lock is emptied and the boat leaves. The confusion that sometimes arises concerns the filling and emptying and which paddles to raise or lower. Remember: Filling is achieved by 'paddles' (think of the bath taps) at the top (higher canal level) end of the lock. Emptying is achieved by paddles (the 'bath plug') at the bottom end. Only one set must be open at one time (taps on and plug out wastes water!). Paddles that are 'Up' are 'Open'.

On the Brecon & Abergavenny Canal the top paddles are 'ground' paddles, operated by rack and pinion gear mounted on the ground on either side of the lock and admitting water via a single central culvert in the stonework below the cill. The paddles at the bottom end are mounted on the gates and let water out through apertures in the gates themselves. At the time of writing some gate paddles are hydraulically operated; others have been replaced by 'traditional' rack and pinion gear.

The lock chambers are approximately 66 ft. long and 9 ft. 6 in. wide. Each lock has a single top gate and a pair of mitred bottom gates. There is a ladder on each side. A footbridge by the bottom gates provides access from one side to the other.

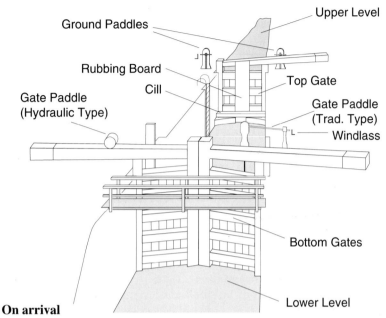

Ground Paddles

Upper Level

Rubbing Board

Cill

Top Gate

Gate Paddle
(Hydraulic Type)

Gate Paddle
(Trad. Type)

Windlass

Bottom Gates

Lower Level

On arrival

- Put the lock crew off, with windlasses ('lock keys'), before entering the lock. If the bottom gates are closed, indicating lock in use, tie up to the mooring bollards provided. Leave at least one person on board to steer!

Going Uphill

- Enter the lock slowly – put the engine astern to bring the boat to rest.
- Position the boat towards the back of the lock, approx. 1 to 2 yards (metres) away from the bottom gates.
- Close the bottom gates; check that the gate paddles are closed (down)
- Open (raise) the top (ground) paddles.

NOTE: Limit turbulence by raising only one top paddle to begin with. Use the engine in reverse, as necessary, to reduce the tendency for the boat to be drawn forward.

- Take great that the bow or fender does not get caught up under any part of the cill or stonework nor, as the water continues to rise, under any part of the top gate.
- When the lock is full, open the top gate and drive slowly out.
- Close the top gate and wind down the paddles.
- Open the paddles on the bottom gates.
- When the lock is empty, open the bottom gates and lower the paddles.

17

Going Downhill
- Close the bottom gates and check that the paddles are down.
- Open both top paddles.
- When the lock is full, open the top gate and lower the top paddles.
- Drive the boat in.
- Position the boat well away from the gates, particularly the top one.
- Close the top gate.
- Open the paddles on the bottom gates.
- Watch that the boat drops freely. If it hangs up drop the paddles at once.
- When the lock is empty, open the bottom gates; wind down the paddles.
- Drive the boat slowly out. Leave the gates open.

TEN SAFETY POINTS FOR CAPTAIN AND CREW

1. **Take your time**
2. **Don't stand on the wrong side of the gate beams** when opening gates (Then you won't be swept into the lock – it sounds obvious but it could happen!)
3. **Do make sure that the safety catch is in position** when raising paddles fitted with rack and pinion gear.
4. **Do hold windlasses firmly on spindles** when raising and lowering paddles. If your windlass slips off the end and hits you it will hurt (greatly)!
5. **Don't leave windlasses on spindles**. If the safety catch fails or is lifted inadvertently the windlass will fly off and injure anyone it hits!
6. **Do watch fingers**, particularly when lowering traditional paddle gear (When lowering, take the strain with the windlass – as if continuing to wind up – lift the safety catch, keeping fingers well clear of rack and pinion, and wind carefully down)
7. **Do keep the boat away from the gates**. In particular:- Make sure when emptying that the rudder does not catch on the cill. Make sure when filling that the bow does not get caught under any part of the stone or timber work.
8. **Do take care if it is necessary to jump on and off the boat**, particularly when the water is below the top level.
9. **Don't take the competence of others for granted**. Remember that safe locking depends largely on those operating the paddles. Be vigilant.
10. **Do watch children**, whether helping or standing by.

IN EMERGENCY, e.g. if the boat gets caught up or someone falls in, **CLOSE ALL THE PADDLES IMMEDIATELY.** This will stabilise the situation and give you time to think.

A busy scene at Brecon

Crossing Brynich Aqueduct

Locking through

Autumn tranquillity near Birdspool

MAPS AND COMMENTARY

STRIP MAPS

16 strip maps cover the 33 miles from Pontymoile to Brecon. The maps are drawn to a scale of 1:25000 (approx. 2½ inches to 1 mile) and there is considerable overlap between each map to allow a useful degree of looking ahead. Each map is angled to show the canal running approximately vertically up the page, so that the line of travel is in line with the guide when laid open on the roof top. A north point is shown as the angle is not constant from map to map.

The scale of the strip maps has been made large enough to enable the canal to be shown in useful detail. Inevitably, many of the geographical features described in the commentary are too distant to be included on the maps. Grid references are given to enable them to be readily located on Ordnance Survey maps, which will be found to be a very useful complement to the guide. The following sheets are required to cover the canal completely (including the Monmouthshire):-

1:25,000 scale
Outdoor Leisure 11; Brecon Beacons National Park Central Area
    or Pathfinder 1062 (SO 02/12)
Outdoor Leisure 13; Brecon Beacons National Park Eastern Area
    or Pathfinder 1085 (SO 01/11)
Pathfinder 1086 (SO 21/31) Abergavenny
Pathfinder 1110 (SO 20/30) Pontypool & Abertillery
Pathfinder 1130 (ST 29/39) Cwmbran
Pathfinder 1149 (ST 28/38) Newport
1:50,000 scale
Landranger Series, Sheet 161: Abergavenny and the Black Mountains
Landranger Series, Sheet 171: Cardiff and Newport
Landranger Series, Sheet 160: Brecon Beacons

COMMENTARY

Adjacent to each strip map is a summary of the principal features of the canal and a list of the facilities available. On the facing pages is a more detailed description of the canal and the countryside through which it passes. This narrative assumes a direction of travel from Pontymoile to Brecon, following the rising sequence of bridge numbers and milepost figures.

19

Inevitably, describing the canal in this way is less than ideal when travelling in the opposite direction. For this reason the description makes reference to views behind, even though the natural tendency when cruising is to concentrate on the scene ahead and on either side. The tendency to look ahead is a distinct bonus since it ensures that the return half of a journey seems almost as if it were on a different canal.

UNITS

With the exception of contours and mountain heights on the maps, where the figures are given in metres in conformity with present Ordnance Survey practice, dimensions and distances throughout the guide are given in Imperial units, the system in which the canal was designed and constructed. Some inconsistency must, however, be admitted, as bridge distances are given in miles and decimal fractions, rather than the more traditional miles and furlongs.

Linear distances given in yards are generally only approximate and it may be assumed that the same figures in metres will be sufficiently accurate. Where a distance is given precisely it may be multiplied by 1.1 to give the approximate number of paces (for a person of average height walking on level ground) or by 0.9 (or, for greater accuracy, 0.92) to convert it to metres.

References to clearances under bridges assume a steel narrow boat with a maximum cabin height above water of approx. 72" and an aft deck 21" above water.

VIEWS AND PHOTOGRAPHY

Frequent reference is made to 'views'. No apology is offered for this. Views may be obvious enough when you reach them but a little advance warning can often be useful. Even at 2 mph it is exasperatingly easy to find that the ideal gap in the hedge has come and gone and the perfect picture been lost because the camera was not to hand at the right moment or a crew member was not available to relieve the photographer from steering. Views may be affected by new tree growth and by the season of the year.

It may be stating the obvious to observe that the time of day is a very important factor. Hills are almost always at their best when the sun is low and a north facing hill scene that looks almost dramatically beautiful in the low sun of early morning can look look singularly unimpressive when seen in shadow in the afternoon. If you are keen to make a good photographic record of the canal and its surroundings it is worth bearing these points in mind when planning your cruise.

KEY TO STRIP MAPS

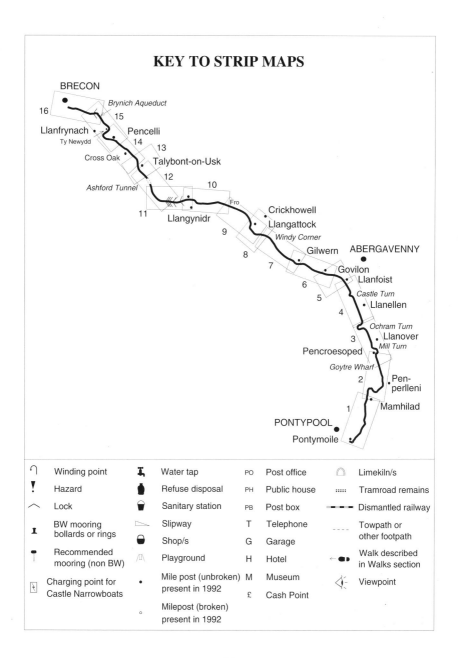

BRECON

16

Brynich Aqueduct

15

Llanfrynach

Ty Newydd

Pencelli

14

Cross Oak

13

Talybont-on-Usk

12

Ashford Tunnel

10

11

Fro

Llangynidr

9

Crickhowell

Llangattock

Windy Corner

8

Gilwern

ABERGAVENNY

7

Govilon

6

Llanfoist

5

Castle Turn

Llanellen

4

Ochram Turn

3

Llanover

Mill Turn

Pencroesoped

Goytre Wharf

2

Pen-
perlleni

1

Mamhilad

PONTYPOOL

Pontymoile

⌒	Winding point	🜸	Water tap	PO	Post office	⌂	Limekiln/s
!	Hazard		Refuse disposal	PH	Public house	::::	Tramroad remains
⌒	Lock		Sanitary station	PB	Post box	═■═	Dismantled railway
1	BW mooring bollards or rings	▱	Slipway	T	Telephone	____	Towpath or other footpath
			Shop/s	G	Garage		
	Recommended mooring (non BW)	�	Playground	H	Hotel	←■▶	Walk described in Walks section
🗲	Charging point for Castle Narrowboats	•	Mile post (unbroken) present in 1992	M	Museum	◁	Viewpoint
		○	Milepost (broken) present in 1992	£	Cash Point		

1. Pontymoile to Mamhilad

Leaving Pontymoile, the canal runs approximately northward, following the line of the mountains to the west and with mainly open views to the east. The rebuilt eighteenth century folly tower (SO295025), is a distinctive landmark. The views from the foot of the tower are superb.

A major dredging programme, started in 2003, has much improved the depth of the canal, particularly in the once difficult length below Jockey Bridge (55)

PONTYPOOL AREA

PONTYMOILE BASIN (52):
Marina Tea Room.
Holiday Cottage (Tel. 07970 548810).
Telephone; 5 mins

SHOPS AND SERVICES (52):
Good range of local shops and services at Windsor Rd., Griffithstown. Follow towpath southward and either cross bridge 50 and turn 2nd left through Broad Street or cross bridge 49 and take 3rd right, through Oxford St.

MAIN SHOPPING CENTRE (52):
15 mins through Pontypool Park

VALLEY INHERITANCE MUSEUM (52):
15 mins through Pontypool Park

LEISURE CENTRE (52):
Pontypool Park; 10 mins.

PUBLIC HOUSES:
Masons Arms, by towpath ½ mile S. of 52
Open Hearth, by towpath 1mile S. of 52
Horse and Jockey (55, 56); 5 mins

MAMHILAD (62)
Church, telephone, post box
The Star

For further information on Pontypool, See page 54

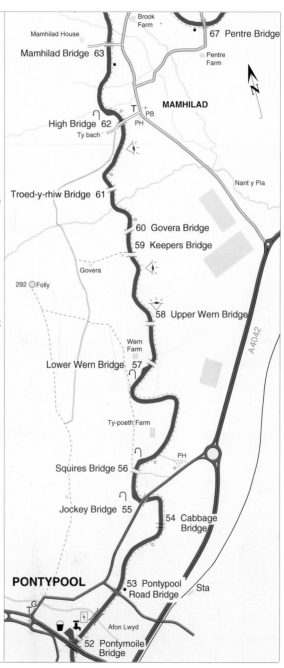

Immediately upstream of bridge 52 is a narrows, formerly a gauging point with stop gates, where boats were gauged for tolls as they passed from one canal to the other. This was done by comparing the draft with measurements recorded under known loading conditions when the boat was first registered. By the narrows is the former toll cottage, now a holiday cottage. Just north of the cottage a footpath leads down from the towpath to the two old tramroad tunnels beneath the canal. To the east lies the site of the tinplate works once served by the tunnels.

Beyond the cottage and tunnels one of the new British Waterways weirs controls the water level on the canal. Surplus water overflows to the Afon Llwyd beneath. You can follow the path down from the towpath to see the aqueduct carrying the canal over the river. North of the aqueduct another path leads down to three more tunnels under the canal, constructed to allow floodwater to equalise, preventing pressure on the embankment.

Shortly before bridge 53 the canal enters a gloomy cutting with, later, houses atop the left-hand bank. Just after the bridge note the 9¼ milepost, one of the Monmouthshire Canal Co. type, placed here after the amalgamation of the two canals in 1865. Four of the type survived in situ on the Brecon & Abergavenny until 1993, differing from the other fractional posts in being much lower to the ground and in showing the total mileage, not just the fraction. A disfiguring iron pipe crosses the canal 200yds above the bridge. As the sides of the cutting fall away, gardens stretch down to the water and a handsome fort graces a play area.

Bridge 54 has long gone. Above the bridge views begin to open up and a gap in the hedge shortly before the canal takes a sharp bend to the left reveals a little hill at Clytha (SO365068). There are monkey puzzle trees and an interesting gazebo/ treehouse in the garden on the bend.

Jockey Bridge, No.55, marks the end of the residential area. The bridge, which is flat and low, takes its name from the Horse & Jockey public house on the main road to the right, adjacent to the church of St. Michael, Llanvihangel Pontymoel. The pub can be reached by road from bridge 55 or by footpath from bridge 56. There is ample room to wind a boat just upstream of bridge 55 and there is also a good winding point 50yds upstream of bridge 56.

100yds further on are the stumps of the cast iron 10 mile post and its later concrete replacement. 40yds after the milepost/s is a less well defined footpath to the Horse & Jockey. After a scramble down the bank, follow the left-hand side of the hedge down across the field. Then either take the overgrown path through the churchyard or continue past the churchyard and take the gate into the road. There is another winding point just downstream of bridge 57.

Above bridge 56 the scenery is pleasantly rural. Ty-poeth Farm stands up on the east side of the canal with its rather ecclesiastical barn windows. Down to the right lies open country with rolling hills in the background and the large roundabout on the A4042 Abergavenny to Newport road in the foreground. Soon, factories come into view on the Usk Valley Business Park and later, particularly on the approach to the bend before bridge 59, on the Mamhilad Park Estate. 100yds before bridge 58 there is a good view left to the folly tower, destroyed in the war as too prominent a landmark and rebuilt in 1994. Gaps in the hedge after bridge 58 give good views forward including a distant view of Ysgyryd Fawr, 1594ft/486m (SO331182). Bridge 59 offers the most direct route for a walk to the folly.

Bridge 60 is an early example of a skew bridge. It is probably no coincidence that William Crosley, the engineer for the extension to Pontymoile, had previously worked under William Jessop on the Rochdale Canal, where some of the first ever skew bridges were built. The arch has been reinforced with bullhead rail, as have a number of bridges nearer Brecon. After the bridge traces of industry gradually fall behind. Bridge 61 was rebuilt in 1951 and now has a flat deck, leaving barely room to stand erect. Visibility is slightly restricted at bridges 60 and 61.

After another attractive open view on the right, the canal enters a short cutting at Mamhilad (Mameye'lad). Steps lead up to the road at the aptly named High Bridge, No.62. Turn right for Mamhilad, a tiny village with telephone box, postbox, church and the Star Inn. The holes where the timber centering was located when the bridge arch was built can still be seen.

There is a nice clean winding point after the left-hand bend above bridge 62. A little further upstream there was once a drawbridge. 200yds before bridge 63 the 12 mile post stood until 1993, one of

2. Mamhilad to Goytre Wharf

Between bridges 64 and 69 the canal makes a major 'wiggle' eastward and for a time the mountains are behind, forming an attractive backdrop. Above bridge 69 the canal turns towards the north once more and there are occasional glimpses of distant peaks ahead. Open meadows and tree-lined edges above Birdspool are followed by Goytre Wharf. Half a mile to the east lies Penperlleni.

MAMHILAD (62)
Church, telephone, post box
The Star

Horseshoe Inn, Pen Croes-hir (65,67,68)
Post box (68)

PENPERLLENI (68, 72); 10mins
Goytre Stores, garage, telephone
Goytre Arms
Goytre Fish Bar
Post office (further 5 mins)

Fresh farm eggs, The Croft (74); 200yds

GOYTRE WHARF
Historic site.
BRITISH WATERWAYS:
Marina, slipway, water point, refuse disposal, sanitary station.
Restored limekilns, picnic area, restaurant, woodland walk, play area, parking. Information, heritage, activity and study centre.
Tel. 01873 881069

HIRE BASE:
Red Line Boats, Goytre Wharf, Llanover, Abergavenny, Monmouthshire NP7 9EW.
Tel: 01873 880516
www.redlineboats.co.uk
Narrowboats, dayboats, canoes for hire. Marine engineers; outboard sales & repairs, fuel, chandlery, gifts, refreshments. Dry dock (not DIY).

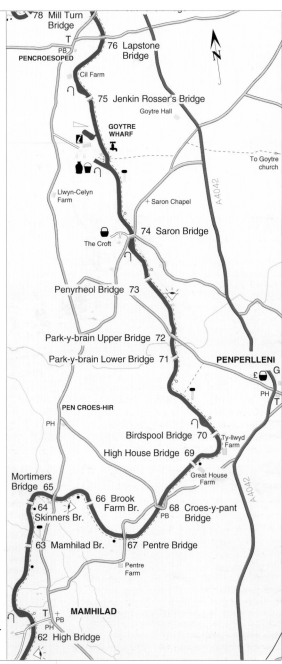

the few true 'mile' posts to survive in situ intact. There are nice open views on the right; bridge 67, nearly a mile away, can be seen on the approach to bridge 63.

The canal is wider and clearer upstream of bridge 63, making a pretty stop for overnight mooring. The moorhen-favoured reed beds, which once obstructed the channel between bridges 64 and 66, are now much reduced. Immediately before bridge 65 is an attractive lengthmans cottage. The canal has turned to run briefly at right angles to the mountains and, once through the bridge, there is a fine view looking back to the cottage and bridge with the mountains behind, best photographed in the morning before the sun moves behind them. The weight restriction notices at the bridge are of LNWR pattern rather than the GWR pattern found elsewhere on the canal.

Views back to the factories occur mid-way between bridges 65 and 66. Shortly before bridge 67 there is a distant view of Mamhilad church on the right. The (12) ¾ milepost, the most northerly surviving example of the MCCo type, stood before the bridge until removed in 1993. Above bridge 67 the canal turns towards the north again and the mountains once more appear to the left.

Between bridges 68 and 72 the canal passes to the west of the village of Penperlleni, which can be reached by road from either bridge. It is possible to moor just upstream of bridge 68. There is a post-box 50yds downhill from the bridge. Penperlleni has a useful general stores with in-store cash machine as well as a fish and chip shop, post office, garage, and telephone box. The Goytre Arms is here; alternatively a pleasant 15 minute summer evening walk up the lane to the west of bridge 68 will bring you to the Horseshoe Inn & Forge Restaurant at Pen Croes-hir.

Boats are moored end-on on the offside at the approach to bridge 69, by Great House Farm. Between bridges 69 and 71, open meadows and tree-lined edges on the offside give the canal an attractive and rather river-like quality. Fine horse chestnuts line the towpath opposite the large winding point above bridge 70. The canal edge is shallow along here making mooring difficult but it should be possible at a lovely tree-lined spot 200yds north of the winding point, shortly before a right-hand bend. Nearly opposite this point a tree-lined area marks a former side pool. A footpath leads from a gate at the back of the towpath through the

edge of a wood to join the road from bridge 72 to Penperlleni, a useful short cut.

Bridge 71 is on a little wiggle in the canal; visibility is slightly restricted. Just before bridge 72 the canal crosses a stream and there is a windlass with the hook for attaching the chain from the drain plug still intact. The bridge is one of many with stop plank grooves. 400yds after bridge 72 and again above bridge 73 there are distant views of Ysgyryd Fawr, with the smaller peak of Ysgyryd Fach (SO316137) on its west side and the peak of Craig Syfyrddin, 1389ft/423m (SO403210), on the other, 12 miles away.

50yds before Saron Bridge, No.74, there is a winding point, somewhat reedy but with the middle apparently usable. The bridge, which takes its name from the nearby Saron chapel, is on a slight bend and visibility is slightly restricted. Fresh eggs and potatoes can be bought at The Croft, 200yds to the west of the bridge; if in doubt, stone cockerels will confirm your destination. Upstream, open meadows and tree lined edges make a brief return.

Soon after, the canal passes Goytre wharf, with restored limekilns, canal buildings, a new inform-ation, heritage, activity and study centre, refresh-ment facilities and a marina, all in a delightful setting. Here too is the base of Red Line Boats.

Purchased in 1810 from John Sparrow, solicitor to the Trent & Mersey Canal Company, the wharf site is well worth a visit. Unless intending to stop only for water – mooring space at the towpath water point is limited – moor south of the side arm, against the towpath where a length of 'post and plank' edging has been provided. Continue on foot to the aqueduct and follow the path down and beneath it into the site. This is also the access route for the sanitary station and rubbish disposal point, which will be found just through the aqueduct arch on the left.

When underway once more, avoid the arm on the left and keep to the right over the aqueduct. As well as the boats moored in the arm and the basin, there is a continuous line up to the next bridge, No.75, and notices remind you to proceed slowly. The canal is for a short while closed in on both sides by conifers; views then open out again before the canal enters a cutting after bridge 76. There is a winding point 50yds upstream of bridge 75. The bend by Cil Farm soon follows, the start of a half-

3. Goytre Wharf to Ty-cochBridge, 84

The course of the canal inclines slightly to the north-west, interrupted by a long anticlockwise semicircle between bridges 76 and 78. The Mill Turn follows immediately – a U-bend where the canal follows the contour round a valley and across a stream; a delightful spot.

Half a mile to the east lies Llanover. There are increasingly frequent views of of the approaching peaks, particularly Ysgyrid Fawr and, upstream of bridge 79, Sugar Loaf and Craig Syfyrddin.

Dredging in 1997 much improved the length from Goytre to Roberts Fm. (88)

GOYTRE WHARF
Historic site.

BRITISH WATERWAYS:
Marina, slipway, water point, refuse disposal, sanitary station. Restored limekilns, picnic area, restaurant, woodland walk, play area, parking. Information, heritage, activity & study centre.
Tel. 01873 881069

HIRE BASE:
Red Line Boats, Goytre Wharf, Llanover, Abergavenny, Monmouthshire NP7 9EW.
Tel: 01873 880516
www.redlineboats.co.uk

Narrowboats, dayboats, canoes for hire. Marine engineers; outboard sales & repairs, fuel, chandlery, gifts, refreshments. Dry dock (not DIY)

PENCROESOPED (76, 77)
Telephone, post box.

LLANOVER (79, 77, 80, 81)
Telephone

NAVIGATIONAL HAZARD
Llanover Bridge (81); arch low at sides.

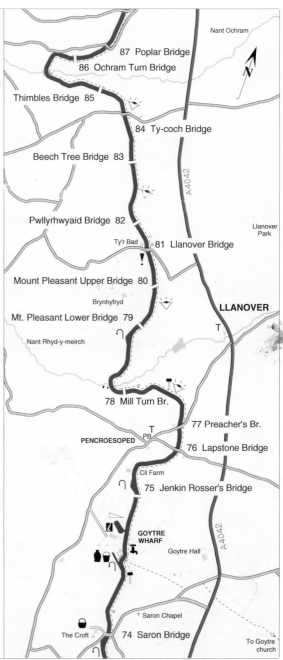

mile anticlockwise semicircle. Dredging has improved this once notoriously shallow bend.

Bridge 76, by Lapstone Cottage, is the stopping point for a 300 yard walk to the hamlet of Pencroesoped where there is a telephone box and postbox. Sadly the general stores has closed. If you decide to dawdle slowly on, fleet-of-foot crew members can leave the canal at bridge 76 and rejoin at bridge 77, which has a nice set of steps up to a stone stile. Above bridge 77 the canal completes its anticlockwise semicircle and begins a clockwise U-bend as it follows the contour round a narrow wooded valley, crossing the Nant Rhyd-y-meirch at the apex. This is the Mill Turn – a delightful spot, ideal for an overnight stop and exploration on foot.

There is a good towpath edge throughout the turn but the views across the valley, to the canal passing round the other side, are best near the ends. If you moor mid-way between bridges 77 and 78, before the start of the turn, you may wake to find yourself bathed in the early morning sunshine that one truly appreciates in Wales. Look over the nearby stone wall at the back of the towpath to see an ingenious feature – a circular cattle trough fed from the canal by a culvert under the towpath. There is a splendid view northwards from here to Ysgyryd Fawr, with the more distant Craig Syfyrddin to its right.

Mill Turn takes its name from Pantglâs mill which stood, with another small building, on the west side of the apex of the bend above bridge 78, about thirty yards from the canal. Remains survive, including the iron sides and axle of the water wheel and a little of the internal machinery.

There is a good winding point 100yds before bridge 79. Sugar Loaf, 1955ft/596m (SO272187), the impressive peak so named from its resemblance to the loaf sugar once sold by grocers, makes its first appearance at the bridge. Llanover, half a mile to the east, can be reached on foot from bridge 79 or, slightly more lengthily, from 80 or 81. There is a telephone box but the post office has closed. In earlier times the post office was the Nags Head but there are no inns today – Lady Llanover converted them into tearooms or coffee houses in the last century! For the desperate, the Goose & Cuckoo stands two miles to the west at SO291073 – well worth the walk from bridges 76, 77 or 81 for the views, beer and food.

From bridges 79 to 85 there are frequent views northward towards Abergavenny and the approaching peaks – Sugar Loaf, Ysgyryd Fach, Ysgyryd Fawr and Craig Syfyrddin. Some of the best views may be seen from: bridge 80 (Sugar Loaf almost dead ahead when emerging), between bridges 81 and 82, when leaving the bend above bridge 82 (Sugar Loaf round to the Skirrids), and from the bend shortly after bridge 84.

Bridge 80 is on the low side with barely room to stand erect. It is also slightly and deceptively skewed to the left so that, when travelling upstream, the towpath appears to project into the channel beyond the bridge hole.

Bridge 81 is very awkward and misleading. The spring of the rebuilt arch is too close to the water. Keep close to the towpath and as you pass through unscathed observe the multi-coloured stripes left by others. When you have successfully negotiated the bridge, notice Ty'r Bad (the boat house) on the left. The minute book of the Brecknock and Abergavenny Canal Committee records that when the canal was completed through to Pontymoile in 1812 the twelve man management committee 'set out to view the Canal towards Pontymoile and at Mr. Waddington's boat house in Llanover, met him, and embarked there on board his Boat ...'. (Benjamin Waddington was the father of the redoubtable Augusta, enthusiast for all things Welsh and husband of Sir Benjamin Hall of 'Big Ben' fame – later Lord Llanover). Take care when passing the private landing stage at the former lengthsman's cottage upstream of Ty'r Bad.

At bridge 82 the towpath edge is 'sandbagged' before and after the bridge; easy for mooring but not ideal because of the approaching bend. If stopping, choose a spot about 75yds upstream, midway between the bridge and the bend.

The approach to bridge 84 provides an attractive forward view between tree-lined banks to Coed y Prior, the wooded hillside at the southern end of Graig Syddi. Upstream of the bridge Llanover church can be seen on the right. From bridges 84 to 85 the lovely view ahead, stretching from Sugar Loaf round to Abergavenny and the two Skirrids, slowly changes as Ysgyryd Fawr begins to slip behind Ysgyryd Fach. Much nearer can be seen Roberts Farm by bridge 88. Less than half a mile away as the crow flies, it is almost a mile by canal and should take nearly half an hour to reach.

4. Ty-coch Bridge (84) to Castle Upper Bridge (95)

Between bridges 85 and 89 the canal takes another U-bend into the hillside, around the Ochram Turn. A much straighter section follows until, above bridge 93, the canal follows the much smaller Castle Turn around yet another valley.

To the east lies the village of Llanellen. The ground has dropped away, the River Usk has come close and there are splendid views towards Abergavenny and the mountains around it.

Bridge 95 marks the start of the first of a number of concrete-lined sections between Llanfoist and Brecon.

LLANELLEN (91, 92)
Church
Post office/stores, craft shop, telephone

LLANFOIST WHARF (Tod's Bridge)
Historic site. See walks section also.

HIRE BASE:
Beacon Park Boats
The Boat House, Llanfoist,
Abergavenny,
Monmouthshire NP7 9NG.
Tel: Abergavenny (01873) 858277
www.beaconparkboats.com
Narrowboat hire
Narrowboat repairs and slipway

LLANFOIST (Tod's Bridge); 5 mins
Post office cum stores
Llanfoist Inn

ABERGAVENNY (Tod's Bridge); 1 m
Good town shops and amenities
including:-
Priory church, castle, museum, leisure
centre.
Market day: Tuesday

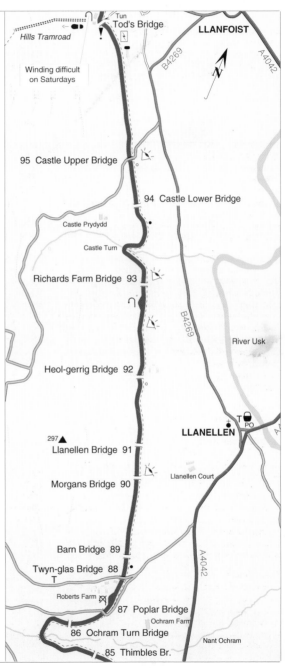

Tun
Tod's Bridge
LLANFOIST
Hills Tramroad
B4269
A4042
N

Winding difficult
on Saturdays

95 Castle Upper Bridge

94 Castle Lower Bridge

Castle Prydydd

Castle Turn

B4269

Richards Farm Bridge 93

River Usk

Heol-gerrig Bridge 92

LLANELLEN
T PO

297▲
Llanellen Bridge 91

Llanellen Court

Morgans Bridge 90

Barn Bridge 89
A4042
Twyn-glas Bridge 88
T

Roberts Farm
87 Poplar Bridge
Ochram Farm
86 Ochram Turn Bridge
Nant Ochram
85 Thimbles Br.

Between bridges 85 and 87 the canal once more contours round a narrow valley, this time the Ochram Turn. Views of the peaks disappear as the canal turns in towards Blaen Ochram and the side of Mynydd y Gárn-fawr while Coed y Prior moves from right to left. Another of British Waterways flood control weirs is sited on the bend, surplus water overflowing to Nant Ochram.

Bridge 86 is flat decked and high. Upstream, there is a nice view down to the stream on the right from the towpath. Moored boats stretch in an almost continuous line between bridges 87 and 88. They intrude into the long-established winding hole and this is no longer an official winding point. Before bridge 88, another flat bridge, the mound behind the house contains remains believed to be an iron foundry in use at the time of the Civil War. It was possibly later used as a lime kiln – a local tramroad built c.1812 connected with limestone quarries at Craig yr Hafod, two miles to the west.

Mid-way between bridges 88 and 89 stood the intact 18 milepost until taken in 1992 (but since recovered). Upstream of bridge 89, Graig Syddi gradually slips behind. The hills diminish and 200yds after bridge 92, the massive bulk of the Blorenge begins to appear beyond them. Ahead and to the west there are intermittent views of the two Skirrids with Ysgyryd Fawr, the larger one, slowly moving to the left of Ysgyryd Fach and emerging from behind it.

Bridge 91 is a flat decked wooden footbridge, leading on the right by footpath to Llanellen village, where there is a post office cum general stores, a craft shop cum tea-room, a telephone and the church of St. Helen. The path is part of the Usk Valley walk, which follows the river from Caerleon to Llanellen and the canal from there to Abergavenny.

A few yards above bridge 92 is an old limekiln, separated from the towpath bank by a narrow track. There is a new winding point 125yds before bridge 93. Between bridges 92 and 93 the river is near and there are further good views, particularly 200yds before bridge 93 and 50yds after it.

After bridge 93, the views of Abergavenny disappear as the canal takes the Castle Turn in and out of the side of the Blorenge, around a small valley. Close to the apex, a stream passes under the canal. A feeder channel supplies water to the canal when required; an overflow weir sends surplus water to the stream in times of flood. There is also a drain plug and windlass. The edging to the towpath is 'sand-bagged' for much of the bend and its approaches but, like the edging generally along the canal, it has fallen away in places as a result of the wash of speeding boats.

Almost hidden from view on the hillside above the canal between the turn and bridge 94 is Castell Prydydd, from which the bend takes its name. Despite the whimsical title – Poets Castle – the site may have ancient origins. The present house was built c.1690.

The canal leaves the turn by a sharp left-hand bend with a good view of the river, which at this point is turning away. The views towards Abergavenny soon resume, being particularly good 50yds after bridge 95. The panorama stretches from the Blorenge on the left round past Sugar Loaf and its three forward reaching shoulders – Mynydd Llanwenarth, Rholben and Deri – to Ysgyryd Fawr and Ysgyryd Fach, with Abergavenny cradled in the middle. Known also as Holy Mountain, Ysgyryd Fawr has at its northern end the remains of St. Michael's chapel, scene of an annual mass at Michaelmas before the Reformation.

At bridge 94, note the grooves worn in the bridge by countless towing ropes. Bridge 95 marks the start of a concrete-lined section of the canal, providing the opportunity to travel slightly faster without fear of causing a damaging wash. For some, it also marks the return to civilisation and the end of the strange sense of isolation that seems to embrace much of the canal below Llanfoist.

150yds upstream of bridge 95, notice the farmer's ingenious water tank on stilts in the field on the right-hand side, which taps water from the canal via a pipe through the bank. Trees now line the back of the towpath and clear views are less frequent. On the left a great bracken covered slope continues until the start of Llanfoist wood, with its splendid beeches.

Half a mile above bridge 95 the canal approaches Tod's bridge, immediately before Llanfoist wharf and boathouse. What is now so quiet and peaceful in its beautiful setting against the wooded hillside was once a hive of industrial activity. Hill's tramroad, constructed c.1825 from Blaenavon round the east side of the Blorenge and down four inclined planes at Llanfoist, linked Hills ironworks at Blaenavon and forge at Garnddyrys (SO257118) with the canal wharf and the Llanvihangel tram-

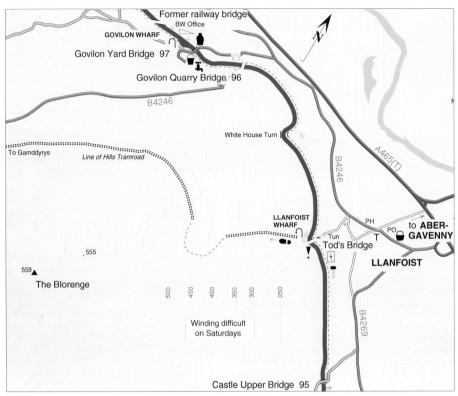

Former railway bridge
BW Office
GOVILON WHARF
Govilon Yard Bridge 97
Govilon Quarry Bridge 96
B4246
White House Turn
To Garnddyrys
Line of Hills Tramroad
B4246
A465(T)
LLANFOIST WHARF
PH
PO
to **ABER-GAVENNY**
Tun
Tod's Bridge
T
.555
LLANFOIST
559▲
The Blorenge
500 450 400 350 300 250
B4269
Winding difficult
on Saturdays
Castle Upper Bridge 95

5. Castle Upper Bridge (95) to Govilon Wharf

Beeches line the hillside on the approach to picturesque Llanfoist wharf. Spread out on the valley floor below lies Abergavenny.

Above Llanfoist the canal turns progressively towards the west as it rounds the Blorenge, the magnificent northern end of the mountain chain that the canal has run alongside since Pontymoile.

Houses and attractive gardens line the outer edge of the canal on the approach to Govilon wharf, head-quarters of the Govilon Boat Club.

NAVIGATIONAL HAZARD
Tod's Bridge; very awkward bend, with hard edges!

GOVILON: See Section 6

LLANFOIST WHARF (Tod's Bridge)
Historic site. See walks section also.
HIRE BASE:
Beacon Park Boats,
The Boat House, Llanfoist,
Abergavenny,
Monmouthshire NP7 9NG.
Tel: Abergavenny (01873) 858277.
www.beaconparkboats.com
Narrowboat hire.
Narrowboat repairs and slipway

LLANFOIST (Tod's Bridge); 5 mins
Post office cum stores
Llanfoist Inn

ABERGAVENNY (Tod's Bridge); 1 m
Good town shops and amenities including:-
Priory church, castle, museum, leisure centre.
Market day: Tuesday

road on the valley floor below. Iron ore by canal from Newport travelled up, wrought iron and finished iron products bound for Newport travelled down, as well as limestone and coal bound for Brecon and Hereford.

The wharf is now the base for Beacon Park Boats but, if you would wish to have conjured in your mind the scene as it was, do read Alexander Cordell's gripping novel *Rape of the Fair Country* and if you would follow in the footsteps of Iestyn Mortimer then read also Chris Barber's *Cordell Country*. A convenient place to moor for an exploration on foot is before the narrows about 100yds downstream of the bridge. This is also the mooring point for a visit to Abergavenny.

Walk through the bridge and down the steps (noting the B&ACCo boundary stone forming the fourth step) to reach the road and the entrance to the tunnel under the canal leading to the tramroad incline. The route of the tramroad can be followed up the hillside, with remains of stone 'sleeper' blocks in places. Alternatively, go down the road to the village of Llanfoist. There you will find the church of St. Ffwyst (St. Faith) where its restorer, ironmaster Crawshay Bailey, lies buried and where a memorial commemorates Thomas Ellwood of Llanfoist, the Brecon Boat Co's land agent – "a faithful servant for thirty years". Also to be found is the Llanfoist Inn and a small post office cum general store.

A mile's walk beyond Llanfoist lies Abergavenny – "The Gateway to Wales" – an important market town with a fine 11th century priory church (noted amongst bellringers for its splendid ring of ten bells), Norman castle (where c.1175 Welsh chieftains were treacherously lured to a Christmas celebration and murdered by William de Braose), historic buildings, museum, shops, leisure centre and numerous watering places.

When you cast off once more, take Tod's bridge slowly and with great care. The bridge is on the sort of bend that just keeps on bending and the problems occur when you leave, not when you enter! If unsure, put a crew member ashore with a bow rope to assist you round. Admire the view over the valley floor as you pass the boathouse. After Llanfoist the canal continues a slow turn toward the west as it rounds the Blorenge. Half a mile beyond the wharf is the White House Turn – look below to see the 'White House'. There are

stop plank narrows and stop gates both before and after the turn to allow this vulnerable section to be sealed off. There was a major breach just downstream of the turn in 1975, followed by a long 'stoppage' while the damage was repaired and two miles of the channel lined with concrete. Earlier breaches of varying severity had occurred in 1812, 1860 and 1914. In 1994 incipient trouble was detected in time and, pending permanent repairs, a temporary steel trough was installed. Travelling through the tunnel-like trough with its brightly painted ends and green roof awning was a novel experience!

Shortly before bridge 96 is the old quarry from which the bridge takes its name. From here to bridge 98 the towpath is on the 'upper' side, altered at the behest of the Llanvihangel Rail Way Company in 1811. To accommodate the change of side without the need to uncouple the towing rope towing horses passed under the bridge on the old towpath before crossing over, or vice versa if heading downstream. The concrete lining of the canal was extended to bridge 98 in 1992.

There is a water point and open-air sanitary station just before bridge 97 and a winding point soon after it, unusually on the towpath side because of the towpath alteration in 1811. The interesting cottages on the right immediately before the bridge were part of Pentwyn farmhouse before their integration into the canal company's 'Abergavenny Wharf'.

The growing wharf complex at Govilon eventually extended as far as bridge 98, near which was the terminus of the Llanvihangel tramroad. Opened to Llanvihangel Crucorney in 1814 and to Hereford in 1819, this tramroad was constructed principally to improve the coal supply to Hereford. It was supplied in part by Bailey's tramroad. Constructed c.1822, the latter ran from Nantyglo via Brynmawr down the south side of the Clydach valley, crossing over the canal by bridge 97, bringing iron and coal for transhipment to the canal and the Llanvihangel tramroad at a point near the old warehouse, which is now a B.W. office. Both tramroads were later largely overlaid by the railways that superseded them, though a small fragment of the Llanvihangel tramroad survives on private property at Govilon.

Approaching bridge 98, there is water point on the offside. Note the 17th century Baptist chapel, one of the oldest in Wales. The former butcher's shop

6. Govilon Wharf to Gilwern

Between bridges 98 and 99 a tight bend takes the canal across Cwm Llanwenarth. To the right, intermittent but impressive views of Sugar Loaf slowly give way to the approaching but still distant mass of Pen Cerrig-calch. At Gilwern, once a complex of individual wharves and tramways, Thomas Dadford's massive embankment carries the canal across the Clydach Gorge.

GOVILON WHARF (97)
Historic site.
Water point, refuse disposal, sanitary station.

CANAL OFFICE:
British Waterways, The Wharf, Govilon, Abergavenny, Monmouthshire NP7 9NY.
Tel: Gilwern (01873) 830328

GOVILON BOAT CLUB:
Slipway

GOVILON VILLAGE (97,98)
Church, 17th century Baptist chapel, post office, general stores, telephone.
Lion Inn, Bridgend Inn.
Water point (98)

NAVIGATIONAL HAZARDS
Humphrey's Bridge 100; very low.
Heads of the Valleys Bridge; blind Z-bend, hard edges.

GILWERN: See Section7

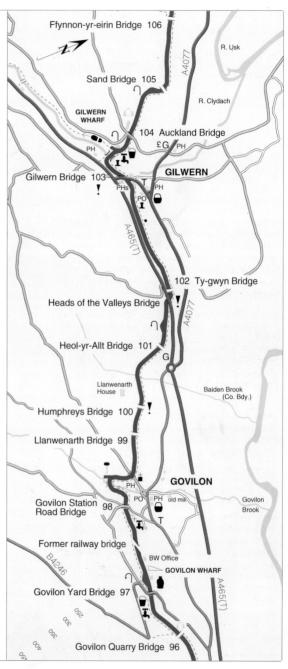

Ffynnon-yr-eirin Bridge 106

R. Usk

A4077

Sand Bridge 105

R. Clydach

GILWERN WHARF

104 Auckland Bridge

£G   PH

PH

GILWERN

Gilwern Bridge 103

PHs   T   PH

PO

A465(T)

102 Ty-gwyn Bridge

Heads of the Valleys Bridge

A4077

Heol-yr-Allt Bridge 101

G

Llanwenarth House

Baiden Brook (Co. Bdy.)

Humphreys Bridge 100

Llanwenarth Bridge 99

PH

GOVILON

Govilon Station Road Bridge 98

PO   PH   old mill

Govilon Brook

T

Former railway bridge

BW Office

B4246

GOVILON WHARF

A465(T)

Govilon Yard Bridge 97

400   350   300   250

Govilon Quarry Bridge 96

by the bridge is now a private house. The road leading down to the main road through the village Govilon (Ger-vye'lon) forks a little below from the bridge. To the right lies a telephone box, to the left a general stores. Further left is a post office, at a junction with the minor road described below.

Soon after bridge 98 note Laurel Cottage, built by William Waters, boat builder, in 1825. The canal now makes a U-turn over the stream coming down from Cwm Llanwenarth, with lovely views behind to the Blorenge. There is an overflow weir and a drain plug and windlass. Immediately beyond the aqueduct is a dry dock, rebuilt in 1992 – a popular overnight mooring. After the turn, another aqueduct takes the canal over a minor road. There are steps down to the road from where you can observe the extremely low headroom – 5ft 6in! Downhill the road leads into Govilon, where the attractions include the Lion and Bridgend Inns and the Victorian church. Built when growing Govilon was created a separate parish from its parent Llanwenarth, the church has the tower placed unusually at the side of the chancel.

Bridge 99, on a slight wiggle in the canal and a trifle awkward, is followed by the flat deck of No.100, Humphrey's Bridge, the lowest on the canal! This bridge leads to Llanwenarth House where the hymnwriter Frances Alexander (neé Humphrey) sometimes stayed. Think of "the purple headed mountain, the river running by" – the Blorenge and the Usk perhaps? – as you pass.

Bridge 101 has a sagging arch, low on the offside. It is at a bend and visibility is poor. There is a small but usable winding point approx. 200yds upstream.

Then follows the bridge built in the early 1960s to carry the new A465(T) Heads of the Valleys road. The canal was re-aligned in an awkward Z-bend under the bridge and it is impossible to see beyond the bridge when entering. It is not easy to take a long boat through without touching and slow speed is recommended. A longish warning blast on the horn before entering is a wise precaution. (Should you receive an answering blast and decide to give way, you will remember that three short blasts is the signal that you are going astern.) Once clear, look back to see the appropriate sign on the road above.

Bridge 102, sagging and reinforced, follows closely after the Heads of the Valleys bridge and marks the start of another section of concrete

lining, completed in 1992. There is a clear stretch with views across fields towards Gilwern Hill on the left, with mast at its eastern end, and through trees and shrubs towards Sugar Loaf on the right and Pen Cerrig-calch ahead.

Gilwern is well worth a visit, not least for its historical associations with the iron making industry in the Clydach Gorge. It has a useful range of shops and services, including a well-stocked general stores, fish and chips, post office (crafts), hairdresser, chemist, surgery and chemist. There is a garage (with cash machine during opening hours) and a generous selection of hostelries, among them the Corn Exchange and the Beaufort Arms.

There are 200yds of moorings on the approach to Gilwern Bridge, No.103, where the Bridgend and Navigation Inns occupy opposite sides of the canal. The final 50yds before the bridge are reserved for the fleet of Roadhouse Narrowboats. By far the oldest boating company on the canal, Roadhouse Narrowboats are in direct commercial succession from Edwin John Goodden, who set up in business as a trader on the canal in 1892.

Gilwern Bridge requires great care. The flat concrete deck is low and on the slope. It is made worse by a projecting pipe part way through. Go slow, aim straight, keep within a few inches of the offside wall and all will be well.

Shortly after Gilwern Bridge another of British Waterways' new weirs passes surplus water under the towpath and down the bank to the river Clydach below. Beyond the weir, a right-hand bend at the start of the Gilwern wharf complex takes the canal across the Clydach Gorge on Dadford's massive 90ft high embankment, constructed in 1797 (Benjamin James of Blaenavon built the aqueduct bridge and the tramroad tunnel; Thomas Powell of Abergavenny and William Watkins of Llanvihangel Talyllyn were the contractors for the earthworks).

On the south side of the embankment was the Clydach Iron Company's wharf, where the Llammarch tramroad, completed 1809, brought down coal from the Llam-march mines and (after completion of the canal to join the Monmouthshire at Pontymoile in 1812) iron from the Clydach ironworks. The route from the ironworks passed the 17th century Llanelly Furnace and Llanelly Forge.

7. Gilwern to 'Windy Corner'

The canal resumes a roughly north-westerly direction. Another concrete-lined section takes it through Gilwern woods. As the trees clear, views to the Llangattock escarpment begin on the left. To the right, Pen Cerrig-calch is the dominant feature.

GILWERN VILLAGE & WHARF (103, 104)

Historic site. See walks section also. Water point, shower block/sanitary station.

HIRE BASES:

Road House Narrowboats,   (103)
50, Main Road, Gilwern,
Abergavenny, Monmouthshire.
NP7 0AS.
Tel: Gilwern (01873) 830240
www.narrowboats-wales.co.uk
Narrowboat hire, repairs, gift shop.

Castle Narrowboats,   (104)
Church Road Wharf, Gilwern,
Abergavenny, Mons. NP7 0EP.
Tel: Gilwern (01873) 830001
www.castlenarrowboats.co.uk
Electric and diesel hire boats, day boats. Water point, pump out, refuse disposal, chandlery and gift shop.

SHOPS AND SERVICES:

Doctor, dentist, chemist, hairdresser, post office, general stores, fish and chips. Telephone, garage.

PUBS:

Bridgend Inn, Navigation Inn, Beaufort Arms, Corn Exchange, Lion

NAVIGATIONAL HAZARDS:

Gilwern Bridge (103); Very low, sloping, projecting pipe.

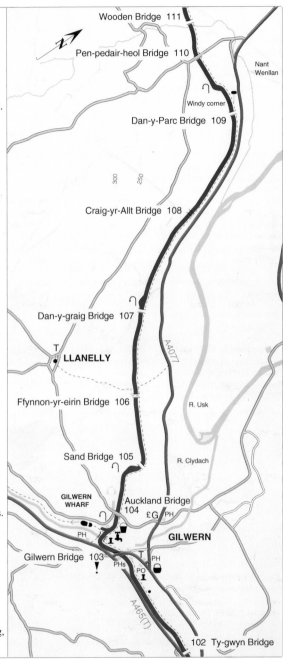

Note the old overflow weir on the bend and the little packhorse bridge crossing it on the path from the wharf. The steps nearby lead up to the A465 and the Lion Inn. There is a drain plug (and was once a windlass) near this point. The weir is still in use, surplus water after heavy rain cascading down an impressive artificial waterfall to the river below.

The concrete lining ends at the end of the embankment. The arm on the left was the Clydach basin. Through an arch at the far end water once entered the canal via a mile long feeder channel from a take-off point on the river further upstream. The public wharf of the canal company stretched along the canal from the basin as far as Church Road. It is now the hire base of Castle Narrowboats. There is a useful chandlery and gift shop, also pumpout and refuse facilities. Water point, shower and sanitary station will be found on the towpath side of the canal opposite Castle Narrowboats.

Through the embankment ran not only the river but also the 1794 Clydach 'railroad' to Glangrwyney, a mile below Gilwern. This was a horsedrawn tramway using bar rails and flanged wheels, similar to modern railway practice, rather than the flanged plateways and plain wheels that later superseded them. Branch lines led to the basin and to further wharves to the east. Down the railroad came coal from Gelli-felen, much of it bound for Brecon; pig iron from ironworks in the Ebbw Vale for the forge at Glangrwyney, and limestone from Black Rock in the Clydach Gorge for road surfacing, for burning locally and for transporting to be burnt in kilns at Brecon.

Mooring is possible on the towpath side of the embankment. Paths and steps link the wharf, the towpath and the railroad tunnel, providing access to the towpath from the other side. The tunnel arch has an unusual step on the south side, the outer arch having been added to carry the Llam-march tramroad. The area is well worth a few minutes exploration, though there are steep banks down to the river and young children should not roam on their own.

Above bridge 104 was the Llanelly wharf operated by the Brecon Boat Company. Buildings erected here c.1802 were later converted into what is now Auckland House. A bank of three lime kilns built by the Boat Company in 1812 survives opposite a parking and picnic area, though trees partly obscure the kilns from view. There is a good view back towards the Blorenge from this point. At the bend upstream of the wharf, before bridge 105, is a large and usable winding point, which would once have been an important turning point for boats using the wharf.

Leaving Gilwern, the canal passes through Sand Bridge, No.105, set on a bend with limited visibility. Nearby sandpits gave the bridge its name. Upstream of the bridge there are good views to Sugar Loaf on the right, at first peeping over a long wooded hill and later towering above the trees.

From bridge 106, an overgrown footpath to the left is worth exploring. It leads to Llanelly church, the parish church of Gilwern. The church has an interesting stained glass window depicting the iron making and coal industries in the area. There are many graves of ironworkers and a memorial tablet in the church commemorates John Powell, the principal proprietor of the Clydach Iron Works for nearly half a century, the memorial erected "by his workmen and friends in affectionate remembrance of departed worth". Sadly, the church may not be open during the day unless arrangements are made for admission.

150yds before bridge 107, another concrete-lined section of the canal commences, taking the canal through Gilwern woods, the upper slopes much denuded by 'harvesting' in 1995. To the left is a steep tree-lined bank, with rocky outcrops in places. To the right, scrubby trees frequently obscure the view. Immediately above bridge 107 is a useful winding point, small but adequate for boats up to 45ft in length. Bridge 108 is no more; only the abutments remain. This flat decked bridge was "in a very bad state ... and quite useless" as long ago as 1862.

As bridge 109 approaches, the end of the wood on the left is reached. Views on the right also open up and 200yds after bridge 109 (at SO223168) there is a good view down the road towards Crickhowell. To the north west, the tower of Tretower Castle (SO185212) can be seen on a clear day. Known as Windy Corner, this spot catches the low evening sun and makes a pleasant overnight mooring point – in calm weather! It is followed by a winding point. A narrows with stop plank grooves at the end of this section of concrete lining marks the site of a former drawbridge.

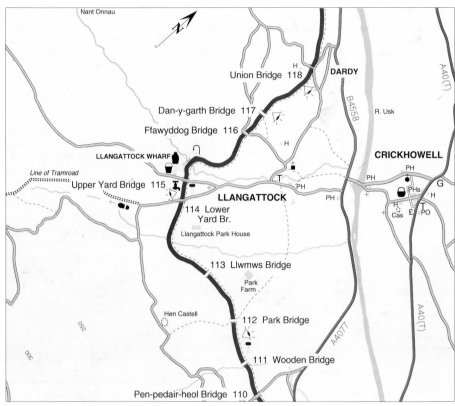

8. Windy Corner to Llangattock Wharf (115)

As Crickhowell approaches, fine views continue; south westward to the quarried escarpment of Mynydd Llangattock and northwards across the Usk valley towards Pen Cerrig-calch. A cutting obscures these briefly as the canal begins a sweep west and then north following the contour around Cwm Onnau, south of Crickhowell. Near the apex lies Llangattock wharf.

LLANGATTOCK WHARF (115)
Historic site. See walks section also.
Water point, shower block/sanitary station.

Llangattock Boat Club

LLANGATTOCK (114,115,116,117,118)
Church
Horseshoe Inn
Vine Tree
Old Rectory Hotel & Golf Course; visitors welcome (116, 117)

CRICKHOWELL (114,115,116,117,118)
Church, castle, 18th century bridge.
Good range of shops and services including post office, bank (Lloyds), cash machine (Nat West), butcher, greengrocer, newsagent, chemist, outdoor gear, ironmonger, gifts.

PUBS AND HOTELS:-
Bridgend Inn, Dragon House Hotel, Bear Hotel, Corn Exchange, Grasshopper, Britannia Inn, Six Bells.

THE DARDY (118)
Ty Croeso Hotel; open to non-residents

Good views continue on the approach to bridge 110 – behind to the receding Sugar Loaf and forwards towards Mynydd Llangattock on the left and the increasingly imposing mass of Pen Cerrig-calch, 2300ft/701m (SO217223), on the right). It was in this section of the canal "near Penpedair Heol" that cutting commenced on Monday, 11th April 1796.

Just before bridge 111, which is flat and high, observe the little stone arch at the back of the towpath and notice that the towpath is lower at this point. The lowering, an 1804 modification to prevent flooding of neighbouring farmland, allowed surplus water in time of flood to flow across the towpath and through the arch to the stream running beneath the canal in a culvert.

Until bridge 110, Table Mountain, the flat topped mound on the flank of Pen Cerrig-calch, has been almost invisible against the background of the mountain itself. Now, as it progressively clears the right-hand edge, it becomes ever more prominent until by bridge 112 it stands completely clear and there is a beautiful view towards it. To the left there are good views towards the Llangattock escarpment; behind lies Sugar Loaf. In good weather, the section above bridge 111 is a delightful, if shallow, spot for those liking an open mooring.

Approaching bridge 113 the canal enters a 200yd long cutting. The original curved line, abandoned in 1803 after a massive breach, is still visible from the back of the towpath at the start of the cutting. Immediately after the bridge there is a fine redwood tree behind the towpath at the beginning of Llangattock Park. A stream passes under the canal on the long bend upstream of bridge 113. The interesting culvert, with its four Romanesque arches, can be seen from a path leading from the towpath near the remains of a windlass, as can the remains of an iron bridge across the stream.

Bridges 114 and 115 are close together and the towpath between them makes a popular overnight mooring spot, with a splendid view of the quarried face of the Llangattock escarpment, a mile to the south. There is a water point on the off side just before new finger moorings and a shower block/sanitary station and rubbish disposal point in the yard by the lime kilns just after bridge 115. Built in 1815 by the Brecon Boat Company, the kilns were restored by British Waterways with a Welsh Development Agency grant in 1995. The Boat Co.

also constructed inclined planes and a tramroad so that limestone could be brought down from the quarries on the escarpment to the kilns. There was a branch to later, now largely demolished, kilns above bridge 114. In later years, a complex system of tramroads developed, linking with the ironworks at Beaufort and, via Bryn-mawr, with Bailey's tramroad down to Govilon. Pit props were shipped out from Llangattock and coal shipped in. The former weighing machine house, now named Westbourne and recognisable by its 'Gothic' windows, survives opposite the entrance to The Chestnuts nursing home – a short walk downhill from bridge 114, which has interesting stone steps set in its face to give access to the road.

The escarpment gives impressive views and is well worth a visit for both its historical and its natural history interest – much of it is now the Craig y Cilau nature reserve. The tramroad route to it from bridge 114 can still be followed. If time is short, ten minutes is sufficient to reach a well preserved length of the stone blocks that once held the 48" lengths of plate rail (SO202167).

Bridges 114 and 115 both give road access to Llangattock and Crickhowell, though the latter can also be reached from bridges 116, 117 and 118. Llangattock is an interesting village, not least for the church of St. Catwg, founded in the 6th century and rebuilt in the 12th. The village stocks are preserved there. Also to be found is the Horseshoe Inn, with a children's playground close by on the opposite side of the road.

Ten minutes walk beyond Llangattock lies Crickhowell. A footpath from Llangattock church leads across fields to the 18th century bridge over the Usk. If walking from bridge 114 or 115, join this path by taking the footpath to the left 50yds beyond the Horseshoe Inn, in preference to remaining on the road. The view across the bridge to Crickhowell is a scene to treasure, with the church of St. Edmund at its centre and Table Mountain, on the side of Pen Cerrig-calch, rising up behind.

Once hailed by its Business Association as 'The Centre of the Universe', Crickhowell is a delightful country town, with much to offer the visitor, including the remains of the 13th century castle built by Sir Grimbald Pauncefoot. Table Mountain, otherwise known as Crug Hywel, the fortified mound of Howell the Good, from which the town takes its name, is even more deserving of

9. Llangattock Wharf to Fro (122)

The next few miles are among the most beautiful on the canal, which resumes its north-westerly course as it passes through the Dardy, entering another concrete section. If one has any soul at all, a late afternoon or early evening journey upstream on a fine day is a memory to treasure. Low sun bathes Pen Cerrig-calch in gold and throws its features into relief, as one passes first Table Mountain, then the craggy outcrop of Darren, and then the end peak of Bryniog, splendid across Glan Usk Park.

LLANGATTOCK
(114,115,116,117,118)
Church
Horseshoe Inn
Vine Tree
Old Rectory Hotel & Golf Course;
visitors welcome. (116, 117).
Water point, shower/sanitary station (115)

CRICKHOWELL
(114,115,116,117,118)
Church, castle, 18th century bridge. Good range of shops and services including post office, bank (Lloyds), cash machine (Nat West), butcher, greengrocer, newsagent, chemist, outdoor gear, ironmonger, gifts.

PUBS AND HOTELS:-
Bridgend Inn, Dragon House Hotel, Bear Hotel, Corn Exchange, Grasshopper, Britannia Inn, Six Bells.

THE DARDY (118)
Ty Croeso Hotel; open to non-residents

NAVIGATIONAL HAZARD
Bridge 121. On a deceptively awkward bend.

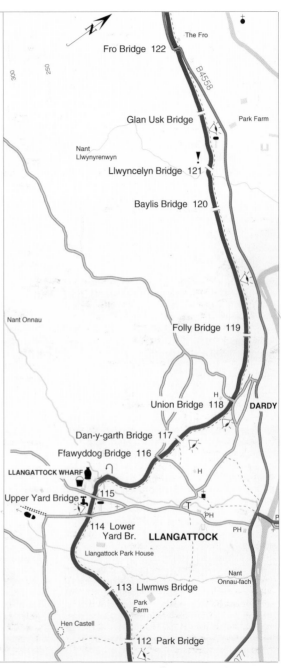

The Fro

Fro Bridge 122

Glan Usk Bridge

Park Farm

Nant Llwynyrenwyn

Llwyncelyn Bridge 121

Baylis Bridge 120

Nant Onnau

Folly Bridge 119

Union Bridge 118

DARDY

Dan-y-garth Bridge 117

Ffawyddog Bridge 116

LLANGATTOCK WHARF

Upper Yard Bridge

115

114 Lower Yard Br. LLANGATTOCK

Llangattock Park House

PH

PH

Nant Onnau-fach

113 Llwmws Bridge

Park Farm

Hen Castell

112 Park Bridge

an expedition and a leaflet detailing the route is available at Crickhowell Adventure Gear in The Square. There is a good range of shops and services (including a cash machine opposite the post office). Crickhowell bridge has thirteen arches on one side and twelve on the other. For those so minded, both the paradox and the view may be contemplated for a while from the Vine Tree, close to the Llangattock end of the bridge. The solution will be found nearer the Bridgend Hotel on the other side.

Returning to the canal and continuing upstream, the wharf by the kilns above bridge 115 is now the base of the Llangattock Boat Club. Beyond the wharf and canal company cottage, built by the Boat Co. in 1821 to house their agent at the kilns, the canal takes a right-hand bend over an aqueduct across the stream from Cwm Onnau. There is a winding point just beyond the apex of the bend. This is adequate for 40ft boats but care is required to avoid the boats moored on the offside and the shallow water along the towpath edge. One of the many GWR round-headed boundary posts can be seen close at hand at the back of the towpath 200yds upstream of the winding point. This example is dated 1917; others include 1891, 1900 & 1920. Marking the boundary of canal company land, all date from after the takeover by the Great Western Railway in 1880.

Views on the left are obscured by rising ground but on the right there are views down through the trees to Llangattock and Crickhowell, best through a brief gap about 200yds before bridge 116. Behind, the Llangattock escarpment remains visible until the bridge. Bridge 116 offers the shortest route to Llangattock and Crickhowell though the most convenient point for mooring, shortly before the bridge, is difficult for deep draughted boats because of the shallow edge. Views on the right across at first Llangattock and later Crickhowell towards Pen Cerrig-calch and Sugar Loaf continue, including clearances 75yds before bridge 117, 200yds after it and 75yds before bridge 118.

Mooring for Crickhowell may be easier above bridge 117. This footbridge is a distinctly private little affair with stairs and a locked door. However, a public footpath leads from a stile by the bridge down the side of the field and across to the gate to join the lane to Llangattock. Between bridges 117 and 118 the canal passes the golf course of The Old Rectory Hotel and Golf Club (visitors welcome).

Approaching Union Bridge, No.118, chimney tops can be seen incongruously peeping over the towpath hedge, for this is The Dardy – a hamlet perched on a hillside. Up on the left and reachable by road from the bridge can be seen the Ty Croeso Hotel. Now highly spoken of and open to non-residents this was once the Crickhowell Union Workhouse from which the bridge takes its name.

Bridge 118 is the last convenient stopping point for Crickhowell. Take the lane leading steeply down from the bridge, bear right at the junction and after 300yds take the footpath across the field on the left towards Crickhowell bridge. There is a rather 'old world' feel to the return walk up the lane. The next concrete section begins at this bridge. The design is not ideal, moored boats tending to grind on the high chamfer.

Continuing upstream, there is now a bank on the left-hand side with rocky outcrops and trees. On the right there are beech trees after bridge 119. 400yds after the bridge, shortly before an overhead line crossing, a very brief clearance gives a good view to the river, here at almost 90 degrees to the canal, with the rocky outcrop of Darren behind.

Between bridges 119 and 122, the canal passes through a pretty tree-lined section above Glan Usk park, primrose scattered in spring and blackberry clumped in autumn, while the river passes on the far side. There are intermittent views through the trees; Pen Cerrig-calch slips slowly by and the Rhiangoll valley opens up around bridge 120.

Bridge 120 has sagged badly and is low on the offside, the first of several such examples along this section of the canal. The arch has been reinforced with bullhead rail. There is insufficient room for the steerer to stand erect. Bridge 121 requires care as there is a bend just before it. Travelling upstream the approach is almost blind; travelling downstream it is all too easy to take the bridge at speed and then find it impossible to negotiate the bend. The concrete edge along this section makes a hard cushion! There is a fine line of oaks above the bridge and down on the roadside can be seen one of the Welsh Water valve houses on the Talybont to Newport water main.

Between bridge 121 and Glan Usk bridge the scrub on the right clears and around Glan Usk bridge there are superb views across Glan Usk farm to the side of Pen Cerrig-calch, ranging from Bryniog at the left-hand end to Darren and Table Mountain on

10. Fro to Llangynidr

Pen Cerrig-calch gradually gives way to the approaching wooded hill of Myarth. This is the first of three hills which over the next seven miles dominate the scene to the north. It is particularly beautiful in autumn with the variegated tints of its mixed deciduous and coniferous trees.

The B4558, never far away, runs close alongside the canal for a while but is almost unnoticed.

As Myarth begins to slip behind, a meandering pastoral stretch marks the approach to Llangynidr, with pleasant views in all directions. Occasional glimpses of Tor y Foel (1800ft) to the west become more frequent.

Post box (126)

UPPER LLANGYNIDR (129)
Church
Red Lion

LOWER LLANGYNIDR (131,132,133)
Telephone, post office, garage
Walnut Tree Stores, 7 days a week
                              (open 'til late)

Coach and Horses (133)

HIRE BASE: (2nd lock)
Country Craft Narrowboats,
Cwm Crawnon Warehouse,
Llangynidr,
Powys NP8 1ND
Tel: 01874 730850
www.country-craft.co.uk
Narrowboat hire

Water point, shower block/sanitary station, refuse disposal.

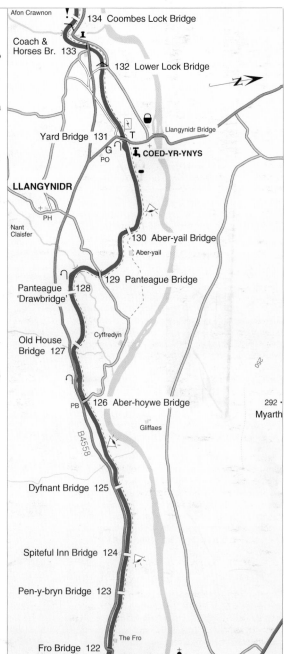

40

the right. Peeping above Bryniog can be seen Pen Gloch-y-pibwyr (SO202232) at the southern end of Pen Allt-mawr. Ahead, the lovely hill of Myarth comes into view on the right, its woodland management plan devised in conjunction with the National Park.

On the approach to Fro Bridge, No.122, the B4558 runs briefly alongside the towpath before crossing the bridge in an awkward double bend. The parapet bears witness to the attentions of passing motorists! The underside of the arch is well reinforced with rail. The bridge sees the end of this concrete section. Soon after the bridge a narrows marks the site of a former drawbridge, where a car can now be parked within inches of passing boats. In the field by the towpath between the narrows and the bridge is a pheasant farm.

To the right, Myarth grows in prominence on the far side of the river, of which there are occasional glimpses, a long field's distance away. There are further blackberry clumps between bridges 122 and 124. Primroses and bluebells are prolific in the spring.

Spiteful Inn Bridge, No.124, probably takes its name from once-nearby Spiteful Inn Farm, which was farmed by the Brecon Boat Company. Just above the bridge is a pleasant spot for a picnic on the bank, though the tree-trunk seats are long past their best. A clearance of about a hundred yards in the trees and scrub lining the back of the towpath provides excellent views to Myarth and back over the end of Myarth to the west side of Pen Cerrig-calch, with Darren at the right-hand end and Table Mountain in the distance.

Trees close in at Dyfnant Bridge, No.125, which has a sagging unsymmetrical arch, low on the offside. Note the paint traces and take care! There is just sufficient headroom for the steerer to stand erect. 100yds upstream of bridge 125 is an attractive but ageing stone barn, with a circular end window and two four-centred arched doorways. Constructed in two stages, the building was possibly once a stables used by the Brecon Boat Company. Recent reroofing, though unsympathetic, has at least helped to preserve the building.

Between bridges 125 and 126 there are good views through the trees across the river to the Italianate twin brick towers of Gliffaes, once a handsome private mansion and now a hotel, set in beautiful grounds at the foot of Myarth. The view is best

near a footpath stile about 350yds above bridge 125, where the river approaches the canal at a bend. Ahead, the bald head of Tor y Foel appears shortly before bridge 126.

There is a postbox at the roadside by bridge 126. For a pleasant three quarter mile walk follow Cyffredyn Lane down from the bridge past Aber-hoywe Farm across Nant Claisfer and towards the river. At a left-hand bend after Cyffredyn either continue on the road to rejoin the canal at bridge 129 or take the public footpath to the right to pass Aber-yail and rejoin the canal at bridge 130.

From bridges 126 to 130 the canal follows a more river-like meandering course in pastoral surround-ings, a pleasant section for an overnight stop. There are winding points 150yds upstream of bridges 126 and 128; the former shallow, the latter recut. On the bend before bridge 127 a substantial arched culvert, visible from the roadside, carries a stream under the canal at a steep angle. The bridge itself requires a little care. (A note in the log reads "struck both head and chimney!"). Bridge 128, very low and flat-decked, was once a drawbridge.

Between bridges 128 and 129 the canal makes a slow and pronounced right-hand bend. At the apex it crosses Nant Claisfer, coming down from the side of Mynydd Llangynidr. Just before the bend is the old overflow weir and just after it the new British Waterways weir that has replaced it. There is a drain plug and the remains of a windlass. Llangynidr church (Llan-gun'idder) is visible from the bend, half a mile to the south-west.

Bridge 129, on a nearly blind bend, is the closest point for Upper Llangynidr, a half-mile walk to the left, where the Red Lion and the church of St. Cynidr, rebuilt in 1873 and again in 1929, may be found. There are good views in almost every direction; westwards towards Tor y Foel, north-westwards towards Buckland Hill and the village of Bwlch clinging to the hillside, north-eastwards to Myarth and eastward back over the stream towards Darren and Table Mountain with Sugar Loaf in the distance. Southwards is Cefn Onneu (SO170163), at the western end of Mynydd Llangatwg.

Bridge 130 also is on a bend with poor visibility. Upstream there is another lovely view eastwards looking back towards Darren, Table Mountain and Sugar Loaf, the perspective heightened by the line of fence posts, the sloping end of Myarth and the

11. Llangynidr

The canal heads west through the five Llangynidr locks, which lift the canal 50 ft. and mark the end of the long pound from Pontymoile. From the first lock there is a fine panorama to the north and east. Before the second, the canal crosses the River Crawnon. Ahead the scene is dominated by Tor y Foel.

The water main carrying water from the Talybont Reservoir to Newport crosses the canal above the first lock. The twin pipes and the attendant valve-houses are visible intermittently from the canal.

UPPER LLANGYNIDR (129)
Church
Red Lion

LOWER LLANGYNIDR (131,132,133)
Telephone, post office, garage
Walnut Tree Stores, 7 days a week
(open 'til late)

Coach and Horses (133)

HIRE BASE: (2nd lock)
Country Craft Narrowboats,
Cwm Crawnon Warehouse,
Llangynidr,
Powys NP8 1ND
Tel: 01874 730850
www.country-craft.co.uk

Narrowboat hire

Water point, shower block/sanitary station, refuse disposal.

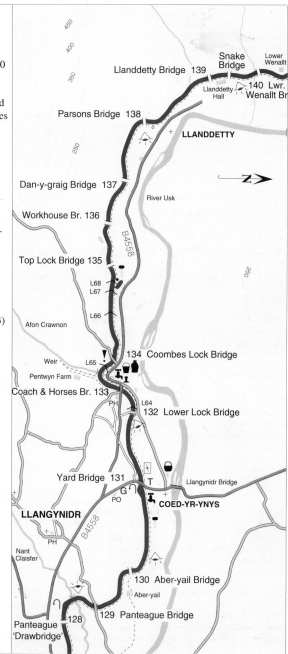

Llanddetty Bridge 139
Snake Bridge
Lower Wenallt
Llanddetty Hall
140 Lwr. Wenallt Br
Parsons Bridge 138
LLANDDETTY
Dan-y-graig Bridge 137
River Usk
Workhouse Br. 136
B4558
Top Lock Bridge 135
L68
L67
L66
Afon Crawnon
Weir
L65
134 Coombes Lock Bridge
Pentwyn Farm
Coach & Horses Br. 133
PH
L64
132 Lower Lock Bridge
Yard Bridge 131
T
Llangynidr Bridge
PO
COED-YR-YNYS
LLANGYNIDR
B4558
PH
Nant Claisfer
130 Aber-yail Bridge
Aber-yail
129 Panteague Bridge
Panteague 'Drawbridge'
128

canal. Ahead, the Usk again draws close giving good views, particularly at a bend in the river 200yds upstream of the bridge.

There is a water point 50yds downstream of bridge 131 and a winding hole opposite. It is possible to moor fairly close in to the towpath edge along here, particularly at a short length of surviving stone edging 100yds before the bridge. There was once a substantial wharf here, with lime kilns in the bank below the canal. Timber products were shipped out and coal and limestone came in.

Yard bridge, No.131, a flat concrete road bridge, is in Lower Llangynidr, also known as Coed-yr-ynys. 250yds uphill from the bridge is a garage and a post office. Just downhill is a telephone box. Nearby was Jones' Timber Yard, from which the bridge took its name. 200yds downhill from the bridge are to be found the Walnut Tree Stores and the ancient and picturesque Llangynidr bridge over the Usk. The 'New' bridge was already old – "ruinous and out of repair" in 1700. There are good views up and down the river from the bridge. The Stores, open seven full days a week, can also be reached by a direct road from bridge 132, allowing shopping for some and locking for others if time is short. Note the upstairs 'windows' of Penlan, opposite the end of Coed-yr-ynys Road.

Lock No.64, the first of the five Llangynidr locks, which are spread over the next three quarters of a mile, is at bridge 132. There are good views from several points. Tor y Foel is particularly impressive looming over bridges 131, 132 and 134, while from the lockside at bridge 132 there is a lovely panorama to the right stretching clockwise from Bwlch past Cefn Moel to Pen Allt-mawr, Pen Gloch-y-pibwr and Myarth. When travelling upstream from the bottom lock there is time for energetic crew members to empty the lock and jog on to reach the next lock before the boat arrives.

Above the bottom lock, rowan bushes, brilliantly berried in summer, line the bank behind the towpath. The twin pipes of the Talybont to Newport water main cross the canal shortly before the rebuilt Coach & Horses bridge, No.133, flat, low and named after the nearby pub. Almost opposite, across the road on the right of the canal, is Boat House, formerly the Boatman's Arms.

There are mooring rings from the bridge to the second lock, No.65. A new concrete lining installed in 1994 had to be replaced in 2001 and 2002 after winter ground water beneath the canal twice caused the bed to lift. A pronounced clockwise bend takes the canal across Cwm Crawnon on the approach to the lock. It is possible to wind a boat on the apex of the bend. There is a drain plug and windlass at the aqueduct.

Before completion of the canal to Brecon, the Crawnon was an important water source. The feeder channel can be followed by crossing the canal at the lock and walking along the side of the river to the sluice, about 300yds upstream. To return, a sharp turn left up the track will lead you past Pentwyn Farm, from where there are good views, to a small junction. A left turn into Castle Road will bring you back to the towpath at the Coach and Horses; a pleasant fifteen minute walk with a popular destination.

Immediately above the second lock, by Cwm Crawnon, is the hire base of Country Craft Narrowboats. There is a water tap, refuse disposal point and a new shower block/sanitary station. Note the long iron strap with hooked end, from an original single-beamed drawbridge, mounted on the wall near the restored warehouse. Bridge 134, just after the waterpoint, is on a bend and slightly tricky; the arch is low and there is insufficient room to stand erect.

A short distance after bridge 134 are the remaining three Llangynidr locks, 66, 67 & 68, in a delightful wooded setting. The top two locks are very close together and a side pond, connected by culvert under the towpath, minimises fluctuations in the water level when a boat locks through. Above the lock there is an attractive mooring spot with picnic tables and a view of Tor y Foel behind bridge 135.

On the apex of the bend just before bridge 136 is the 'old workhouse', which was later a pair of farmworkers cottages and is now a private house set in beautiful gardens. A scene fit to grace a chocolate box, it is best photographed from just upstream and late in the day to catch the sun. Bridges 136 and 137 are both on slight bends with limited visibility.

Upstream of 136, the canal wiggles its way along the side of Tor y Foel, with a lovely sweep of tree-lined hillside rising up in front as the canal takes a bend to the right 150yds above bridge 137. Allt yr Esgair appears on the right as the canal works round Buckland Hill and turns towards the north. Midway between bridges 137 and 138, Llanddetty

12. Llangynidr to Talybont

Above Llangynidr the canal passes along the flank of Tor y Foel and turns briefly north, before the Ashford Tunnel. To the right, Buckland Hill, just reaching mountain status at 1038 ft, has replaced Myarth as the principal feature. There are good views eastward along the Usk valley. After the tunnel, the wooded ridge of Allt yr Esgair (1287ft) grows in prominence, standing above the canal-side village of Talybont.

Dredging has much improved the once shallow section between Llangynidr and Ashford tunnel, particularly approaching bridge 138.

TALYBONT (142,143,144)
Historic site. See walks section also.

DAYBOAT HIRE (142):
Brecon Boats, Counting House,
Talybont-on-Usk, Brecon,
Powys. LD3 7YP.
Tel: Talybont (01874) 676401.
Dayboats, 3-5 seats

SHOPS AND SERVICES (143,144):
Talybont Stores & Post Office;
Drawbridge Coffee Shop and Tea Rooms. (open seven days a week)

PUBS AND HOTELS:
Travellers Rest (142)
Star   (143)
White Hart (143)
Usk Inn, Station Rd. (143)

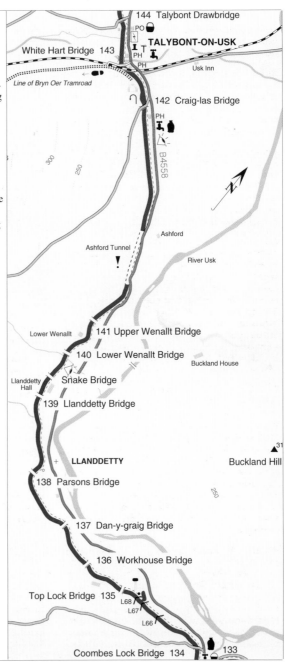

144 Talybont Drawbridge
White Hart Bridge 143
TALYBONT-ON-USK
Usk Inn
Line of Bryn Oer Tramroad
142 Craig-las Bridge
PH
300
250
B4558
Ashford
Ashford Tunnel
River Usk
141 Upper Wenallt Bridge
Lower Wenallt
140 Lower Wenallt Bridge
Buckland House
Llanddetty Hall
Snake Bridge
139 Llanddetty Bridge
LLANDDETTY
Buckland Hill
138 Parsons Bridge
250
137 Dan-y-graig Bridge
136 Workhouse Bridge
Top Lock Bridge 135
L68
L67
L66
Coombes Lock Bridge 134
133

44

church (at SO128202) can be seen down in the valley ahead, with Buckland Hill and Allt yr Esgair behind.

Bridge 138 has a modern Bailey bridge above the original arch, erected by the Forestry Commission to facilitate harvesting the conifers on the hillside above. The canal below 138, once notoriously shallow due to soil run-off from the denuded hillside, has been much improved by dredging.

Between bridges 137 and 139 there are good views looking eastwards back down the valley. From the bend 150yds upstream of bridge 138 a valve house on the Talybont to Newport water main can be seen on the roadside below. Streams run into the canal along this section and there may be shallow points where sandbars have formed.

Approaching bridge 139, there is an oblique view of the front of 17th century Llanddetty Hall, built by Jenkin Jones, one of Cromwell's colonels and a signatory to Charles I's death warrant. In the 19th century it was for a time owned by George Overton, the tramroad and colliery engineer, and later by Mary Anne Wyndham Lewis, who married Benjamin Disraeli. Across the Usk Valley two distant peaks – Mynydd Troed and Mynydd Llangorse – can be seen between Allt yr Esgair and Buckland Hill, with a fine view sweeping round from Allt yr Esgair to Sugar Loaf.

From bridge 139 past Snake Bridge, a low and flat bridge with bellied iron T-beams, to bridge 141, there are pleasant views towards Buckland Hill and the derelict suspension bridge which crosses the river to Buckland House at the foot of the hill. Views of the bridge are perhaps best midway between Snake Bridge and bridge 140. To the left of the canal, the flank of Tor y Foel spreads round in a great arc, as the canal slowly passes under the side of Wenallt. An excellent sweet chestnut tree overhangs the towpath 100yds before bridge 140. Once ripe, the chestnuts seem to disappear almost overnight!

Bridge 140 is on a slight bend and deceptively awkward. It is followed by a deceptively sharp, and once shallow, bend at 'monkey-puzzled' Lower Wenallt. Bridge 141 has a reinforced arch but is more or less symmetrical. Buckland House itself, once a British Legion home and now a Conference Training and Residential Study Centre, is best seen 150yds above bridge 141. The view is particularly lovely in the autumn. There are further nice views eastward down the valley from between bridges 140 and 141.

Quarter of a mile above bridge 141 is the 375yd (343m) long Ashford tunnel. There is no towpath; in working days horses went over the top and boats were worked through manually. There are gauge boards at the tunnel ends and a water level indicator just downstream. About a third of the way through, from the downstream end, there is a kink and a dip and the roof comes down to within a few inches of the top of the boat!

Don't forget your headlight and don't enter unless the tunnel is clear. It should be your aim to pass right through without touching. The best approach is to stand in the centre of the rear deck sighting over the top of the roof and lining the boat up for the centre of the arch where it dips. For the lowest few yards you may well not have headroom to stand erect – duck or grouse! Take it slowly, particularly at the lowest point. There is a ventilation shaft exactly half way. Any crew members not wishing to travel through the tunnel can walk over the top and find the ventilation shaft. There they will be able to hear the boat throughout its passage through the tunnel and discern with amazing clarity the voices of those on board.

Upstream of the tunnel the ground on the right progressively drops away as the canal approaches Talybont-on-Usk, passing through it on an embankment some feet above the road.

Shortly before bridge 142 is the Travellers Rest, adjacent to the towpath and with moorings for patrons. A water tap and disposal facilties for bagged rubbish are available at the start of the moorings. Opposite are the dayboats of Brecon Boats. A former warehouse beyond the Travellers Rest is now an attractive cottage; the large patio door facing the canal makes an effective mirror if you wish to photograph yourself passing. The views of Allt yr Esgair are splendid from here and continuing upstream. There is a postbox on the road by bridge 142.

100yds above bridge 142, a concrete replacement for an earlier girder bridge, itself a replacement for the original, the canal widens out into a basin formed by Jonathan Dixon in 1814 when the limekilns were being constructed. You can see where he put the excavated soil! There should be room between the reeds to wind a boat. By the kilns was the wharf of the 'Brinore Tram Road'.

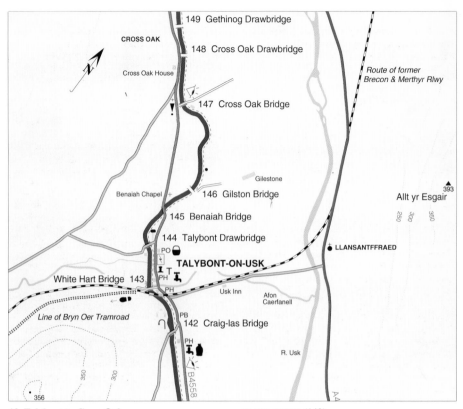

CROSS OAK

149 Gethinog Drawbridge

148 Cross Oak Drawbridge

Cross Oak House

*Route of former
Brecon & Merthyr Rlwy*

147 Cross Oak Bridge

Gilestone

Benaiah Chapel

146 Gilston Bridge

▲ 393
Allt yr Esgair

145 Benaiah Bridge

350
300
250

144 Talybont Drawbridge

PO

● LLANSANTFFRAED

TALYBONT-ON-USK

White Hart Bridge 143

PH

Usk Inn

Afon
Caerfanell

Line of Bryn Oer Tramroad

PB

142 Craig-las Bridge

PH

R. Usk

350
300

B4558

• 356

13. Talybont to Cross Oak

The canal passes through Talybont on a concrete lined embankment, crossing the Afon Caerfanell and passing beneath an electric drawbridge.

After Talybont, the canal leaves Tor y Foel and Wenallt behind and runs along the north-east shoulder of Bryn. Across the valley, Allt yr Esgair in turn recedes, and views open up across meadows and river to Mynydd Troed, Mynydd Langorse and more distant hills of the Black Mountains.

The Taff Trail from Cardiff to Brecon joins the towpath at Talybont and walkers enjoying the trail may be encountered on the final seven miles to Brecon.

TALYBONT (142,143,144)

DAYBOAT HIRE (142):
Brecon Boats, Counting House,
Talybont-on-Usk, Brecon,
Powys. LD3 7YP.
Tel: Talybont (01874) 676401.
Dayboats, 3-5 seats

SHOPS AND SERVICES: (143,144)
Talybont Stores & Post Office; Drawbridge Coffee Shop & Tea Rooms (open seven days a week).

PUBS AND HOTELS:
Travellers Rest (142)
Star   (143)
White Hart (143)
Usk Inn   (143)

NAVIGATIONAL HAZARD
Bridge 147; On an awkward bend, particularly travelling upstream.

This opened in 1815 and ran for 12 miles from the Bryn Oer colliery near Rhymney via the Trevil limestone quarry. Coal came down for Brecon and, via the Hay tramway, for Kington and Hay. Pitwood went back up to the collieries. The line of the tramroad can be seen as a terraceway in the field between the limekilns and the approaching railway bridge. The route of the tramroad southward can be reached from bridge 143 and makes a pleasant walk, with good views of the Talybont reservoir.

The water pipes from the Talybont reservoir to Newport can be seen once again, this time crossing the canal shortly before the railway bridge, which once carried the former Brecon & Merthyr Railway. Bridge 143, reinforced but not noticeably sagging, follows 40yds after the railway bridge. Due to the narrowness and shallowness of the channel there is an appreciable downstream current through the bridge.

Above the bridge, the canal bends to the right and crosses the Afon Caerfanell on a narrow aqueduct. The bend makes the approach to the bridge awkward when travelling downstream. There is a water tap behind the towpath, 15yds upstream of the bridge. It is awkwardly sited on the bend, but with care just sufficient room can be left for another boat to pass. On the offside is an overflow weir at the start of the aqueduct; also a drain paddle. The approach to the weir can be used with care to wind a 40ft boat.

At the foot of the canal embankment lie the White Hart and the Star, from the beer gardens of which, particularly the latter, are views of the aqueduct. There are public conveniences and a telephone box near the White Hart. The long red-bricked building, with tethering rings for the former street market, was built in 1903 as tea rooms. The Usk Inn will be found in Station Road, five minutes walk towards Llansantffraed.

A major breach in the embankment 100yds west of the aqueduct in December 1994 caused serious local flooding, particularly in the Star. The 300yd section up to the approaching Talybont draw-bridge, No.144, was reconstructed with a concrete lining. Shortly before the bridge note the old canal company cottage on the left, with the initials B&ACCo between the first floor windows. Below the embankment to the right is the Talybont Stores cum Post Office and Drawbridge Coffee Shop &

Tea Rooms, open seven days a week. Prior to the restoration of the canal in 1970, through navigation had been prevented by a fixed bridge at this point, installed in place of an earlier wooden drawbridge. The present steel drawbridge is the second since 1970.

The bridge is electrically operated, using a standard BW 'Watermate' key and 'raise' and 'lower' buttons. There are clear instructions on the control pedestal. A public road crosses the bridge and gates must be closed before the bridge can be raised. Make sure they are fully secured when closed, and again when opened (i.e. vertical bolts fully home). Note that the key cannot be removed until the gates have been opened. Keep well to the offside when passing through. The clearance is limited and the site is exposed to the wind. Notices on the bridge state the times on school days when it should not be raised, currently 8.00-8.45 a.m. & 3.15 to 4.00 p.m. Sadly, the local school closed in April 1991; the roll had fallen to three.

Observe the tapping rails at the towpath edge when passing under bridge 145. Care is required when travelling downstream if alighting here to prepare for opening the drawbridge. The approach to bridge 146 is particularly pretty on a bright autumn day, when sunlight gilds the multi-trunked beech tree beyond the bridge. Quarter of a mile above bridge 146 at the end of a long left-hand bend, the right-hand bank falls to give views across open farmland towards the first manually operated lift bridge, No.148, at Cross Oak. To the left the canal is skirting the lower slopes of Bryn. Behind are Wenallt and Tor y Foel, particularly attractive in the lovely mixed colours of autumn.

On the bend approaching bridge 147 is a pair of old cottages. In summertime it is worth a brief pause at the bridge to walk a few yards down the lane and admire or photograph the rose covered front of the cottages and the view across the Usk valley to 'The Allt'. The bridge requires care; it is on a right-hand bend and the arch, though symmetrical, is rather low with only just sufficient headroom for the steerer to stand erect – witness the paint left by others!

In the angle of the road junction on the left can be seen Cross Oak cottages and a war memorial cross. The name is older than the cross and appears in Welsh on the 1883 OS map. On the west side of the junction is a tree-lined rectangular enclosure

14. Cross Oak to Pencelli

The canal continues north-westward along the lower slopes of Bryn in a pleasant pastoral setting. Hedges line the towpath, with fields, the river and distant hills beyond. Three manually operated drawbridges (148, 149 & 150) add variety on the approach to Pencelli 'castle' and village.

PENCELLI (153,154)
Telephone box, post box
Slipway
Royal Oak

LLANFEIGAN (154, mile)
Church

LLANFRYNACH (158, mile)
Church
White Swan

HIRE BASE AND MARINA (159):

Cambrian Cruisers, Ty Newydd,
Pencelli, Brecon, Powys. LD3 7LJ
Tel: Llanfrynach (01874) 665315
www.cambriancruisers.co.uk

Narrowboat hire.
Repairs and painting.
Dry dock (not DIY).
Pump out, diesel fuel, gas.

Cambrian Marina. Tel. 01874 665478
Brokerage and moorings.

NAVIGATIONAL HAZARDS
Bridge 147; On an awkward bend, particularly travelling upstream.
Bridge 156; deceptively low

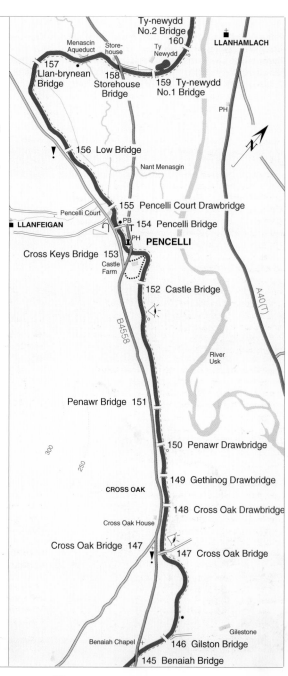

within which stood the 'Iron Church' – a corrugated-iron chapel of ease to Llanfeigan church built c.1880 to serve Cross Oak and demolished c.1970. Further upstream, the gardens of Cross Oak house have fine displays of azaleas and rhododendrons in late spring.

Ahead can be seen bridge No.148, the first of a group of three manually operated drawbridges. Bridges 149 and 150 follow soon after. Bridge 148 is usually found open; the others closed. All should be left as found. The bridges have suffered from much redesign over the years. Until 1982 they were raised by pulling a chain hanging from the counterweighted end of the top beam, a simple and effective system copying the original design. A dreadful wire and bobbin arrangement followed before the installation of hydraulic gear, operated by the standard windlass. Recent 'improvements' to the hydraulic design have introduced towpath operation and a higher opening angle, but at the expense of very greatly increased effort. Each bridge now takes from 80 to 100 turns to raise, compared with about 40 formerly. Some care is advisable to align the boat correctly when passing through to avoid leaving the task to the massive and unyielding timber fendering which will otherwise perform the task for you!

A good technique is to drop a crew member or members at bridge 147 to go ahead to raise and lower 148, 149 and 150 in turn as the boat passes, reboarding 300yds further on at bridge 151. (The bridges are pivoted on the offside. It is courteous not to drop a bridge if another boat is approaching, even if your 'winder-upper' may thereby be delayed and have to walk after you to rejoin the boat – next time you might be the beneficiary!)

50yds after bridge 148 notice an unusual sight on the left – a branch of one tree appears to have grown right through the trunk of another. 50yds before the second drawbridge, No.149, the tip of Mynydd Troed, 1997ft/609m (SO165202), can be seen over the falling foreground on the right, peeping to the left of the receding Allt yr Esgair. More of the range comes into view further upstream. Trees and shrubs line much of the towpath between bridges 151 and 153 but there are occasional brief views across the river and the hamlet of Scethrog to Mynydd Troed and Mynydd Llangorse (on its right), for example by an overhead line crossing 50yds upstream of a stop plank narrows, 200 yds before bridge 152.

Bridge 151 is the best point for putting off a crew member to operate the drawbridges when travelling downstream. Note the painted number 13 on the upstream keystone, the clearest survivor of the original numbering sequence, which started from Brecon. Traces can be seen on other bridges.

Above bridge 152, as the canal bends to the left, take a breath of history, for you are now cruising through the moat of Pencelli Castle. Apart from the original motte (mound) of the once significant castle, little now remains except the gaunt farmhouse and buildings that have used its stone and taken its name. One of a string of castles built by the Marcher Lords and their followers to maintain control of land taken from the Welsh, Pencelli's subsequent history of ownerships and surrenders was as much concerned with rivalry between the kings of England and their barons as with attempts by the Welsh to regain control.

Shortly after Cross Keys Bridge, No.153, named after a pub which once stood nearby, the canal passes the Royal Oak, a popular watering place with good mooring facilities. There is a telephone box and a postbox on the north side of bridge 154. Just upstream of the bridge is a slipway and a large winding point. Beyond the slipway, a narrow road to the left leads to Llanfeigan church (SO086245), popular with visiting bellringers because of the excellent tone of its bells and its isolated location. Armed with an OS map and/or a guide to walking in the Beacons, it is possible to reach the Beacons from here via the footpath past the church and the path over Bryn. A one-way journey to the principal peak, Pen y Fan, 2906ft/886m (SO012125), takes about 4 hours walking time.

Just beyond the winding point and slipway, by Pencelli Court Farm, is the final drawbridge, No.155. Upstream of the bridge, a long line of moored boats requires passing with care. This is a very pleasant 'leafy' section of canal, with open fields, lowish hills and tree-lined edges. Mynydd Troed and Mynydd Llangorse continue in view intermittently on the right until, above bridge 157, rising foreground begins to obscure them.

Bridge 156 has a symmetrical but deceptively low arch – much too low for lying on the roof or for the steerer to stand erect. Black mink may be seen along this section of canal.

As the canal sweeps round the long bend between 156 and 160 the scene before you rapidly changes.

15. Pencelli to Brynich

After Pencelli and the last of the manually operated drawbridges (155), the canal makes a sweeping clockwise detour between bridges 155 and 160.

Above bridge 156, glimpses of the principal peaks of the Brecon Beacons begin to appear, culminating in superb views near bridge 160. Rising ground for a time then obscures them. The river is now very close, with good views through the trees at several points.

The two principal peaks visible are the pointed crest of Crybin (2608ft) and, to its right, the flat topped peak of Pen y Fan (2906ft).

LLANFRYNACH (158, mile)
Church
White Swan

HIRE BASE AND MARINA (159):

Cambrian Cruisers, Ty Newydd, Pencelli, Brecon, Powys. LD3 7LJ
Tel: Llanfrynach (01874) 665315
www.cambriancruisers.co.uk

Narrowboat hire. Dayboat hire.
Repairs and painting.
Dry dock (not DIY)
Pump out, diesel fuel, gas.

Cambrian Marina. Tel. 01874 665478
Brokerage and moorings.

GROESFFORDD (163, 10 mins)
The Three Horse Shoes

NAVIGATIONAL HAZARDS
Bridge 156; deceptively low.

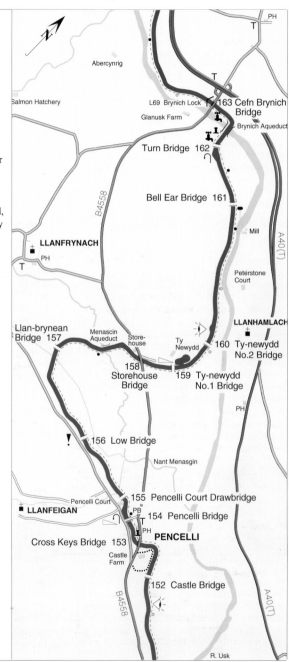

To the west there are various views towards the Beacons, including good views of Pen y Fan from around bridge 157. The bridge is flat, low, on a bend and slightly awkward, with insufficient room to stand erect.

400yds above bridge 157, the canal crosses Nant Menascin. For some years this was the narrowest part of the canal, the aqueduct having been rebuilt to 8ft. 6in. width when the canal was out of use and navigation unimportant. It was rebuilt in concrete in 1992 and the width increased to approx. 11ft. 9in. Sections of 19th century Barlow's patent rail and GWR broad gauge rail were recovered during the rebuilding. A stile leads down to the stream, from where there is a good view of the aqueduct. Kingcups grow in profusion on the wet ground to the east of the aqueduct in springtime.

The White Swan at Llanfrynach, noted for its food, can be reached by a three quarter mile walk by road from bridge 158. The village centre is a pleasant composition, with chapel, church and inn set in a square.

Just before bridge 158, is the old Storehouse, built by Rees Williams in 1825. For some years this housed the Water Folk Canal Centre; a fascinating and beautifully presented museum of canal history, now sadly closed. The boathouse at the side arm by the bridge was built by the canal company.

There was once a winding point immediately after the bridge. Looking back from further upstream there is an attractive view southwestwards to Pen y Fan framed between trees over the bridge. Look south to the hillside below Bryn to see if you can spot Llanfeigan church tower, submerged in a dip on the hillside with the belfry louvres apparently at ground level. To the south-east there is a good view along the Usk valley. Pencelli Castle farmhouse stands out on the right with Allt yr Esgair on the left and Buckland Hill in the distance.

Immediately above bridge 159 is the marina at Ty Newydd and the hire base of Cambrian Cruisers. Diesel fuel and pump out are available. (You can moor for the latter at the jetty upstream of bridge 159, immediately before the marina entrance.)

Approaching bridge 160, Llanhamlach church can be seen to the right. The bridge itself is flat decked and low with insufficient room to stand erect. Some of the best views of the Beacons are to be seen from around this bridge, perhaps best of all

about 100yds on the upstream side, near the remains of an old windlass. The post and plank edging above the bridge makes for convenient mooring.

Rising ground on the left soon obscures the Beacons but offers instead an interesting craggy bank. On the right, Llanhamlach church and Peterstone Court Hotel are prominent above the far bank of the river. Keep your eyes open when approaching the overhead line crossing – the eagle eyed may be able to see the remains of the suspension towers of a footbridge that once crossed the river at this point. Look back from here towards Llanhamlach for a good view of the river.

250yds before Bell Ear bridge, No.161, there is an inviting little quarry on the left, primrose scattered in Spring. (possibly the 'quarry in Balia wood' noted in 1813). Soon after there is a fine view on the right down to the river and the old mill. This is a pleasant mooring point for an overnight stop where one can drift off to sleep lulled by the distant babbling of water over the rocks in the river below. The mill has been restored and converted into a distinctly desirable residence. Trees prevent an unobstructed photograph from the canal. A footpath leads down towards the river's edge (reachable also from bridge 161) which can be followed along the river to Brynich aqueduct, returning via the towpath in a pleasant twenty minute circular walk.

Bridge 161 has a sagging reinforced arch, low on the offside. Above the bridge the river veers away slightly but there is a good view from the canal about 400yds after the bridge. The Beacons reappear on the left as the foreground again. Just before bridge 162 – almost invisible on approach but immediately past the last tree on the left – there is a useful winding point, more than adequate for a 48ft boat.

Bridge 162 requires a little care as the canal bends to cross the river via the Brynich aqueduct. The towpath turns over at the bridge and remains on the south side for the final two miles to Brecon. British Waterways' contractors carried out major repair works on the aqueduct in the 1996/97 winter. Ancillary works included the provision of a water tap and mooring bollards on the approach to the aqueduct and this a mooring popular spot. Just before the aqueduct a now redundant drain plug, chain and windlass is on display

16. Brynich to Brecon

At Brynich, the canal crosses the River Usk on a substantial four-arched aqueduct, followed shortly by Brynich lock. Above the lock, the water is deeper and clearer and the bottom of the canal can be seen for much of the way into Brecon. The widened towpath is now the Brecon to Brynich Cycleway.

Intermittent views of the Beacons give way to a splendid panorama on the approach to bridge 164.

The terminus of the canal has been greatly enhanced by a major regeneration scheme, completed in 1997, comprising two new basins and an adjacent theatre complex, funded by Powys C.C. with a Strategic Development grant from the Welsh Office.

Telephone (163)

GROESFFORDD (163, 10 mins)
The Three Horse Shoes

BRECON (165,166, 167)
NEAR WATTON BRIDGE (165):
Garage (groceries)

NEAR GASWORKS BRIDGE (166):
Water, shower block/sanitary station,
refuse disposal.
Regimental museum.

NEAR DADFORD BRIDGE (167):
Baker/Newsagent; top of Conway St.
(filled baguettes)
Children's playground.

THEATRE BASIN (167):
Theatr Brycheiniog.
Dragonfly Cruises: Trip boat and day
boats. Tel: 07831 685222

TOWN CENTRE (167, 5 mins):
Good town shops and amenities
including:-
Cathedral, parish church of St.Mary,
Brecknock Museum, cinema.
Swimming pool (mile).
Numerous public houses and hotels.

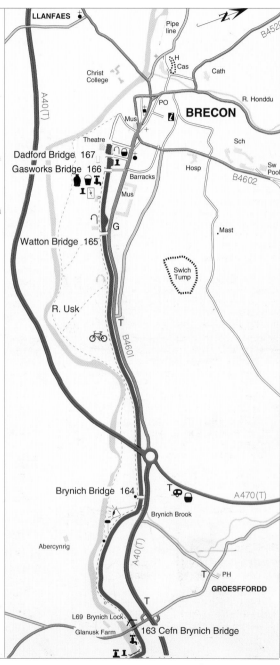

52

From the aqueduct there are good views of the river and of the ancient Brynich bridge. For a low level viewpoint, walk down from the offside of the canal to the river's edge to see the aqueduct itself and, through its arches, the bridge beyond. They are seen at their best fairly early in the day, when the sun is shining on the face of the bridge and the aqueduct.

Brynich Lock follows soon after the aqueduct. There is nice worm-drive paddle gear at the top end on the offside. The 'Draw forward' tendency is strong in this lock. While waiting for it to fill, notice Brynich bridge, which photographs part-icularly well from this angle in late afternoon sunshine. The bridge itself is a good vantage point from which to photograph the aqueduct. There is a telephone box on the main road, the A40, three minutes walk from the lock. At Groesffordd, ten minutes walk north from the junction, can be found the Three Horse Shoes.

From Brynich Lock to Brecon the towpath was widened and resurfaced in the 1997/98 winter to form a cycleway. There are good views to the river, now on the left. Pen y Fan is briefly visible from the picnic area just above the lock. Views of the Beacons improve as the trees clear and between Abercynrig Farm, on the far side of the river, and the bend downstream of bridge 164 there is a splendid panorama spreading westward from Bryn to Cefn Cyff and on to Crybin and Pen y Fan. This is a fine spot for an overnight mooring. Along this section Pen y Fan's flat- topped sister peak, Corn Du, 2863ft/873m, can just be seen peeping briefly past the western edge of Pen y Fan. This is the only point on the canal from where Corn Du is visible. Ahead is a brief foretaste of Brecon.

Sheltering under the arch of bridge 164 for a hundred years stood the (40) ¾ milepost, until its theft in 1993. Shortly after bridge 164, the canal passes under a new bridge, 70yds long, carrying the Brecon bypass. The Brynich Caravan Park shop can be reached from here by a five minute road walk from the A40/A470 roundabout.

From bridge 164 on, the Beacons are progressively lost to view, hidden by the long conifer-clad hill which dominates the view to the south on the approach to Brecon. The river moves away and open fields and playing fields increasingly fill the foreground. To the right, the road into Brecon flanks the canal, though it is rarely obtrusive.

Behind can be seen Allt yr Esgair and, in the distance, Pen Cerrig-calch. Compared with what has gone before, the final section into Brecon can seem slightly monotonous.

300yds before bridge 165 was an extensive stone edged wharf. There is a long bank of limekilns in the bank behind the towpath, invisible from the canal but accessible on foot by walking back down the lane from the bridge. To the right of bridge 165 is the Slwch Tump, site of an ancient fort. Note the overgrown second arch. Through this once passed the Hay Tramway, which opened in 1816 and ran from Brecon to Hay, carrying coal outward and farm produce back.

There is a good winding point about 100yds above bridge 165. Midway between bridges 165 and 166 can be seen the remains of the 42 mile post against the front of 'Brecon Canal Guesthouse'. There are moorings approaching bridge 166 and just before the bridge there is a water point with sanitary station, shower block and rubbish disposal facilities. At the bridge itself there is a good view forward over the tower of St. Mary's church to Pen-y-crug, 1088ft/331m (SO028303).

Beyond bridge 166 the canal passes through 'Probert Basin'. The widening on the right is roughly on the site of an 1801 basin, which later gave entry to the Boat Co's side arm.

To the left of the new Dadford bridge. No. 167, is a children's playground. To the right, Conway Street gives easy access to Jones the Baker and News-agent at the junction with the Watton.

Through the bridge lies the Theatre basin, with *Theatr Brycheiniog* facing the attractive front gardens of Cwrt Conway across the water. This is the terminus of the canal. From here the trip boat Dragonfly operates (public trips Wed, Sat, Sun, Easter to November; charter hire by arrangement). There are mooring bollards in both basins and room to wind a large boat in the theatre basin.

Water from the River Usk flows into the basin through an culvert in the end wall, piped through the town from a weir half a mile upriver. The canal originally continued along the line of the present road for a further 200yds, with an arm on the right ending near the fine four-storey brewery warehouse dated 1892 in Danygaer Rd.

PONTYMOILE

Junction Cottage, Pontymoile

Pontymoile marks the end of the Brecon and Abergavenny Canal and it is well worth making the effort to get this far, even if you are not intending to continue into the restored section of the Monmouthshire.

There is in any case more to Pontymoile than meets the eye. Apart from the immediate scene around the side basin just below bridge 52 with the Marina Tea Room and the old toll cottage (now a holiday cottage), the attractions of Pontypool are within easy reach. Less than half a mile away is Pontypool Park, where there is an excellent swimming pool and leisure centre. Beyond the park lies the main shopping centre and the Valley Inheritance Museum, which has a canal display and is well worth a visit.

The basin is on the line of what was once the continuation of the Monmouthshire canal to Pontnewynydd. The basin is leased out but entry for turning, water (there is also a tap by the narrows above bridge 52) or using the sanitary station is permitted. Take care to keep away from the shallow slipway.

The entrance is narrow. Boats less than about 45 ft in length will find it possible to turn by entering bow first and no further than necessary to allow the stern to be swung round in the line of the canal. However, boats longer than about 45 feet, will find this impracticable and may find it necessary to reverse into the basin, turn within the basin, and reverse out with the stern heading downstream.

Mooring:-
Apart from the space reserved at the charging point for electric hire boats,

there are no designated visitor moorings. However, you may moor temporarily at any empty landing stage on a 'grace and favour' basis; alternatively moor against the towpath if you can get within convenient plank distance, either above bridge 52 or through the road bridge below bridge 52.

Things to see:-

Just north of bridge 52 is the former toll cottage and the narrows (once a level stop lock) where boats were gauged. A little beyond the cottage a path leads down the canal embankment from the towpath to two old tramroad tunnels beneath the canal. The tunnels ran from the site of a former Tinplate Works on the east side. It is possible to walk through one of the tunnels and turn left up rough steps to return to the basin via the landscaped area. Children in particular may enjoy this little piece of exploration.

A little further up the towpath from the toll cottage is the aqueduct where the canal crosses the Afon Lwyd. A well fenced path leads down to the river's edge and gives a good view of the aqueduct and river. There are further tunnels, built to prevent flood pressure on the embankment, north of the aqueduct.

To reach the leisure centre:-

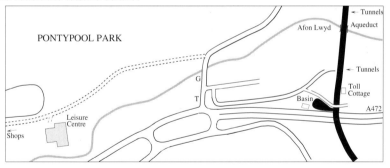

Take the track leading out of the back of the basin and bear left into Fountain Road. Follow the road as it bears right past the fountain and turn left to a T-junction. At the T-junction turn right, cross the road, pass the Esso Garage and turn left through the gates of Pontypool Park.

The gates are a bare 5 minute walk from the basin; the leisure centre is a further 5 minutes walk through the park. To reach the shopping centre and the museum continue on past the leisure centre. Where the path forks, bear left for the shops or right for the museum, which is housed in the stable block of Pontypool Park House at the far end of the park.

BRECON

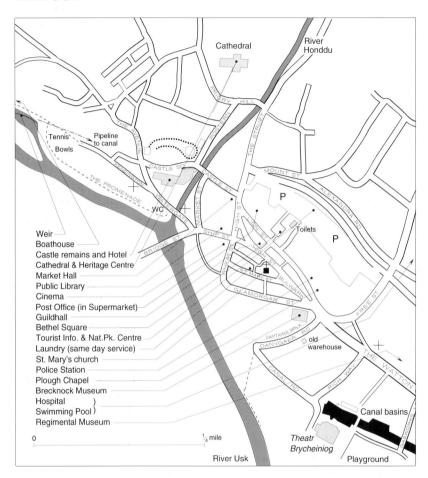

Tennis
Bowls
Pipeline to canal

Cathedral

River Honddu

Weir
Boathouse
Castle remains and Hotel
Cathedral & Heritage Centre
Market Hall
Public Library
Cinema
Post Office (in Supermarket)
Guildhall
Bethel Square
Tourist Info. & Nat.Pk. Centre
Laundry (same day service)
St. Mary's church
Police Station
Plough Chapel
Brecknock Museum
Hospital)
Swimming Pool)
Regimental Museum

0   ¼ mile

River Usk

Theatr Brycheiniog

Canal basins

Playground

old warehouse

Toilets

Brecon is a busy market and borough town, seat of the diocese of Swansea and Brecon and centre for the Brecon Beacons National Park. Granted its charter in 1246, it still retains something of its old-world atmosphere, complemented by good shops, pubs, restaurants, hotels and modern facilities. Amongst its many attractions for the visitor are the Brecon Swimming Pool and Leisure Centre, Brecknock Museum, the Regimental Museum of the South Wales Borderers and the internationally renowned Brecon Jazz Festival, held each year in August. Significant recent additions are the Bethel Square shopping development and the *Theatr Brycheiniog* at the end of the canal. The theatre and the new canal basins, funded by Powys County Council with a Strategic Development grant from the Welsh office, have enhanced the area. Demolition of the nearby abattoir has also helped to remove the down-town feel that once characterised arrival in Brecon by canal.

The church of St. Mary, the 12th-14th century cathedral church of St. John the Evangelist, raised to cathedral status in 1923, and the 19th century interior of the Plough Chapel of the United Reformed Church in Lion Street are amongst Brecon's architectural treasures. An intriguing, if trifling, puzzle is the purpose of the small stone structure across the basin from the theatre. It is probably no more than a 19th century gazebo but alternative suggestions include a signal office, used for controlling boat traffic.

The tower and curtain walls of the ancient Norman castle can be viewed from the gardens of the Castle of Brecon Hotel. The area was known to the Romans and Brecon lies on the route of a Roman Road to the fort at Y Gaer, 3 miles to the west.

Brecon Weir (½ mile)

To reach the weir, from where the canal draws its water, walk into the centre of the town. Keep to the left of Lloyds Bank and follow Ship Street downhill towards the river. Do not cross the Usk but just before the bridge turn right into Watergate and cross the much smaller bridge over the River Honddu. Turn left by the side of the public conveniences and walk down to the path along the river – the 'Promenade'. Look beneath the Honddu bridge to see, exposed in the river bed, the cast iron pipe through which water flows to the canal. Return to the Promenade and follow the path westward along the bank of the Usk. It is a pleasant walk with fine views southwards to the principal peaks of the Beacons. In quarter of a mile the river divides. Follow the path as it swings round to the right and the weir will soon be seen, together with the settling pond and sluice, where water enters the pipe to the canal. To return, turn right along a path leading into Kensington and back to Watergate. Manhole covers on the route of the pipe can be seen at intervals. Standing by the manhole nearest the sluice, the sound of rushing water can be clearly heard.

The Boathouse

A few minutes further along the Promenade beyond the weir is the 'Boathouse', a popular amusement and refreshment centre where the hire of splashcats and rowing boats are among the attractions on offer.

CANALSIDE FURNITURE

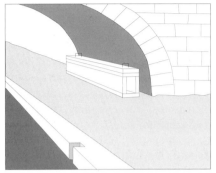

STOP PLANK GROOVES AND PLANKS

At many bridges, and a few other points, there are stop plank grooves. These vertical slots allow planks to be dropped in on edge, one above the other, to isolate a section of the canal for repairs, maintenance or to contain a leak. The planks are often stacked nearby in readiness.

WINDLASS

PLUG AND CHAIN (not seen)

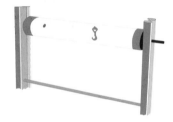

At a number of points along the canal, the remains of windlasses can be seen. Near each windlass, set deep in a masonry-lined hole in the bed of the canal and covered with clay to complete the seal, is a drain 'plug' and chain. When it was necessary to drain a length of canal, the chain from the wooden plug was connected to a hook on the windlass roller and bars inserted into holes in the roller to wind out the plug and chain, allowing the water to flow through the drain into a nearby watercourse. The plugs can still be used though the windlasses are no longer used to draw them out.

MILEPOSTS

There were once cast iron mileposts at quarter mile intervals along the canal. Many broken stumps still survive but almost all the intact posts were stolen in 1992/3, the remainder being removed by British Waterways for safe keeping. The milepost positions date from after the amalgamation of the Brecon & Abergavenny Canal with the Monmouthshire and indicate mileages from Llanarth Street, Newport, almost exactly 9 miles south of Pontymoile.

Near Pontymoile there were examples of the stubby Monmouthshire Canal Co. type, transplanted to the Brecon & Abergavenny from the Monmouthshire. These showed the total mileage to the nearest ¼ mile.

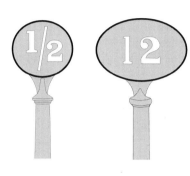

Brecon & Abergavenny posts showed the mileage total only at the true 'mile' posts. Quarter-mile posts carried just the fraction.

BOUNDARY POSTS

Posts marking the canal boundary were erected by the GWR at various dates after their takeover of the joint canal in 1880. The supports are old broad gauge rail.

WEIGHT RESTRICTION NOTICES

GWR weight restriction notices can be seen at many bridges. Unusually, the plate at bridge 65 is of LNWR pattern.

BRECKNOCK & ABERGAVENNY CANAL Co.

The initials of the canal company can be seen on canal property at several points along the canal.

B & ACC°
1843

WALKS

The directions given below are based on notes made on location by the author and should prove adequate to enable the routes to be followed. However, a 1:25000 or 1:50000 O.S. map would be a useful aid, as would a slight sense of adventure. For additional information on features of interest or alternative and extended routes, refer to publications listed in the Bibliography.

A proper degree of care and supervision of young children is required, particularly on steep hillsides and near quarry faces and industrial remains. If you take refreshments or a picnic, please take your litter away. Don't leave it to injure livestock or spoil the countryside for others.

All the walks follow existing paths and can be undertaken in 'sensible' shoes. However, some parts are rough and others may be wet and muddy in bad weather. Walking boots are recommended.

The times are on the generous side, Brisk walkers not intent on admiring the view will be able to shorten them by at least quarter of an hour. All distances are approximate.

WALK 1: THE FOLLY

A pleasant walk with one steep field to climb, rewarded by fine views stretching from Sugar Loaf in the North to the Transporter Bridge at Newport in the South.

Starting Point: The towpath at Bridge 56   **Time**: Allow 1¾ to 2¼ hours
Distance: 3½miles   **Height climbed**: 580ft/180m

(Note: A far more direct route starts at Keepers Bridge, No.59. Cross the bridge and follow the waymarked footpath path past the right hand wall of the cottage. Continue ahead across the field and bear right when you reach the farm buildings. Continue forward with the farm buildings on your left and when abreast of the farm house bear right into the drive. In approx. 100 yards turn left into a roughly metalled track. Continue along the track for approx. 400 yards and then take up the instructions at the point asterisked in the directions below.]

From the towpath, cross bridge 56, cross the stile at the far side of bridge and turn immediately right, signposted Circular Walk Public Footpath, into a loosely metalled track. 50 yards after passing Ty-poeth farm buildings on the right continue straight ahead on the track and ignore the gate on the left. After open fields on both sides the track meets the canal at a bend. Continue ahead, past a "Private Property No Vehicles ... Footpath Only" sign.

After 50 yards, immediately before a gateway across the track, turn left over a stile, clearly waymarked "No. 2", into a field.

The O.S. map shows the path heading approx. straight ahead and then slightly left to the far left corner of this quarter-mile long field. However, depending on the state of cultivation it may be preferable to follow the left hand edge of the field (ignoring the gate in the left hand fence)

At the far corner of the field cross the stile, waymarked No.2. Ignore the second stile immediately on your right and head uphill, past a small cattle drinking pool, with a fence to your right. There are increasingly fine views looking back towards Newport including the Transporter Bridge.

At the top of the field there is a stile on the right. Cross this stile and continue for 10 yards to a roughly metalled track. (*)

Cross the track (briefly right and left) and over another stile (waymarked "Circular Walk Public Footpath No.2"). In approx. 15 yards cross another stile and continue uphill across the field, heading at first for a clump of scrubby trees on the ridge ahead. The folly soon appears 45° to the right.

As you near the trees veer slightly to the right, passing a waymark post, to the stile that will now be visible. Cross this stile, signposted "Circular Walk No.2" and "Public Footpath" and continue uphill across the next field (i.e. do not head directly towards the folly). The next stile will soon be in sight. Cross it when you get there and turn right into the track to the folly.

To return to the canal via Mamhilad retrace your steps to the track at point * *(above)*. Then turn left and follow the track back to Mamhilad at bridge 62.

To return to the canal via Pontymoile, re-enter the track by which you reached the folly. Ignore the stile where you joined the track on the way up and continue straight ahead – now a narrow green lane with hedges, mainly ferny and with some views through the gaps. There are frequent yellow waymark arrows pointing the way ahead. In due course, pass a little repeater station on your right, the track becoming a little rougher and stonier. At a staggered cross roads continue straight ahead, later bearing slightly left past the entrance to a house (Pen y Parc). At a gate and stile continue ahead, now crossing an open field with a parallel wall on your right. At the far side continue straight ahead through another waymarked gate. The track becomes a sunken green way and then, after crossing another waymarked stile, gets narrower, sinuous and rougher, with large, loose and uneven stones. In due course, emerge through the kissing gate into Usk Road, opposite P and P Cars. Turn right pass the main entrance to Pontypool Park and in 100 yards cross the road by the Esso Garage (Pontypool Service Station) and turn left into Fountain Road. Continue to the canal basin at Pontymoile, rejoin the towpath and walk north for a mile to bridge 56.

WALK 2: LLANFOIST TO GARNDDYRYS FORGE

The initial section involves a steepish climb and rough walking up the route of the inclined planes of Hill's Tramroad. Thereafter the going is good and the walking easy. There are fine views.

Starting Point: The towpath at Llanfoist Wharf   **Time**: Allow 2½-3hours
Distance: 4½miles   **Height climbed**: 860ft/260m

Take the steps leading down from the towpath at Tod's Bridge, noting the old B&ACCo boundary stone now forming the fourth step, and turn right through the tunnel under the canal and the wharf cottage. Follow the track of the tramroad up the hillside, keeping to the right of the stream. There were originally three inclined planes here and stone sleeper blocks, often displaced from their original positions, can be seen in places. Here and elsewhere can be seen traces of coal that has fallen from the wagons.

In approx. 350 yards continue straight ahead (actually slightly right and left) by a small brick hut and after another 100 yards cross a stile. In a further 50 yards cross a track (signposted left to Lower Pen-y-Graig and right to Upper Pen-y-Graig) and continue ahead, signposted Cwm Craf.

In a little over 100 yards, at a junction of fences, ignore the waymarked stile and gate on your right, but note it for possible use on your return journey (*) and continue up the hill side to another stile visible approx. 100 yards ahead. Cross this stile and continue ahead. There are good views looking back.

In a further 100 yards the fence on your right turns sharply away to the right. Follow it briefly as it turns and then veer slightly leftwards towards the top end of the stone wall ahead of you. Turn right at the end of the wall to rejoin the track of the tramroad, which for the rest of the route round the northern slopes of the Blorenge is clear and unmistakable. Many stone sleepers remain in position and there is even a 50 yard long tunnel (which looks usable although the path now bypasses it) and there are excellent views.

100 yards after the far end of the tunnel a waymarked path leads down on the right, beside a fence and wall, towards a coniferous wood. Note this for possible use on your return journey. (†)

When you reach the B4246, turn left for 100 yards and then take the track on the right by the electricity 'H' pole into the site of Garnddyrys Forge. Chris Barber's *Cordell Country* is an invaluable guide to the remains and to further walking and exploration in the area.

To return to the canal you can retrace your outgoing steps. Alternatively, follow the road downhill towards Abergavenny and in approx. 1 mile, where the road bends sharply to the left, continue straight ahead into a narrow hollow way. Follow this through the wood to bridge 96. Cross the bridge and turn right along the towpath for Llanfoist. However, there is no separate footway beside the road and it cannot be said that this is a very safe or pleasant route.

A more pleasant, if slightly more adventurous, return route is to retrace your outgoing steps from Garnddyrys as far as the path leading down towards the coniferous wood described above *(see † above)*. Take the path but when you reach the wood DO NOT cross the stile into it but instead turn right and walk along the top edge of the wood outside the fence. Cross the stile in the wall ahead of you (120 yards) and continue ahead, passing through an open gateway in another fence in approx. 200 yards. Continue straight ahead, passing by a stunted oak tree in approx. 50 yards. The edge of the wood is now curving away to your left but eventually swings back. Where you meet it, after about 150 yards, take an obvious path leading downhill through the wood. When you meet a stile cross it, ignore the gully continuing downhill and bear slightly to the right and (at first) slightly uphill through a less wooded area. In approx. 300 yards, at the lower corner of another wood, you will reach a junction of walls and fences by a low beech tree, with a stile on your left. Cross the stile into a narrow field and continue briefly straight on. At the far side of the field, ignore the gate, turn right and follow the track along the long side of the field until you arrive back at the gateway mentioned earlier *(see * above)*. Turn left down the incline to return to the canal.

WALK 3: GILWERN WHARF TO CLYDACH IRONWORKS
This is a pleasant walk passing several features of historical interest. There are fine views across the Clydach valley on the return journey.
Starting Point: The towpath at Gilwern   **Time**: 1½ to 2 hours
Distance: 3¼miles

Go through the tramroad tunnel under the Clydach embankment on the bend opposite Castle Narrowboats. Just after the second of two cottages (Aqueduct Cottage and the former weighing machine house on the Clydach Railroad), ignore the rising line of the Clydach Railroad and fork left through a gateway, following the line of the Llammarch tramroad. After ½ mile, by Forgehammer sewage pumping station, note the footbridge across the River Clydach on your left. (Your route lies straight ahead but make a brief detour to see the river and waterfall.)

In due course note Forge House on your left. Immediately abreast on your right is the site of Llanelly Forge. (There is a signposted path to the top of the wall of the old dam, from where you can see the remains of the pond). Pass through Forge House gateway to join a lane, making a mental note of the gateway for the return journey.

Continue past converted ironworkers cottages on the left, emerging into a minor road at a bend. Keep straight on but first look right towards another bend with the site of Llanelly Furnace on its left and 17th century Clydach House, where 'The Clerk to the Furnace' lived on its right.

In 200 yards continue ahead on the minor road, i.e. ignore the junction with the Heads of the Valleys Road on the left. After a further 400 yards take the steps or slope on the left (just before a junction with a road coming down from the right) and pass through the pedestrian tunnel under the main road. On the far side turn right.

In 150 yards the path passes through a gate and meets the river at a small stone bridge. Do not cross the bridge but instead continue along the right-hand bank for 75 yards to Smart's bridge, a small but attractive cast iron structure dated 1824. Turn left over this bridge to the remains of the Clydach Ironworks (c.1793-1861).

After viewing the remains, take the incline uphill to the right of the ironworks. Bear right through Dan y Coed housing estate, forking right through Dan y Coed Bungalows to take the footbridge across the Heads of the Valleys Road, from where there are good views down the valley.

On the other side, bear immediately left up a flight of shallow steps. At the top of these turn briefly right (i.e. do not go immediately left down to the school) and then pause for a decision. If tiring, continue to the right to join the road and resume the directions at the next paragraph. Alternatively, turn left before the row of interesting buildings in front of you onto the route of the Clydach Railroad, c.1794. Continue for about 300 yards and then, by the decaying remains of a red brick double garage, turn right up a path and steps to the Merthyr to Govilon turnpike road c.1812. Turn right into the road, from where there are good views across the valley.

Follow the road downhill through 'Cheltenham', passing several interesting buildings and an end-wall display of enamel signs, for about a mile (¾ mile if you omitted the last section). Near the bottom, where a lane leaves the road and heads uphill to the left, rejoin your outgoing route and retrace your steps to the canal.

WALK 4: LLANGATTOCK ESCARPMENT

This route includes a steep walk up an inclined plane but is well worthwhile. Features of interest include the tramroads, the quarry faces and the views. If time is short, barely five minutes level walking will suffice to bring you to a well preserved length of stone sleepers.

Starting Point: Bridge 114   **Time**: 2 to 2½ hours
Distance: 3¾ miles   **Height climbed**: 700ft/210m

From bridge 114 take the road toward the escarpment. After 350 yards, where the road bears sharply left, climb over the stile on the right of the bend; walk forward 10 yards and turn left on to the route of the old tramroad.

Follow the line of the tramroad, in 200 yards noting the fine length of stone sleeper blocks still in place as you approach a gate. These once held the iron rails, along which horses pulled the loaded wagons from the foot of the inclined planes on the hillside ahead. Pass through the gate, ignore the waymarked stile immediately to the left, and continue ahead. A further ½ mile will bring you to a stile at the foot of the first inclined plane. The wagons loaded with quarried limestone ran down under gravity, drawing up empty wagons in their place. At the top of this incline – a steep scramble but well worth the effort – are the remains of the pit for the brake wheel and beyond it a seat for admiring the view while you regain your breath. From the top of the incline, turn half left up another incline, slightly narrower, to the tramroad track along the escarpment.

From the top of the second incline there are many possibilities for further exploration but if you wish to return to the canal from this point you can turn left along the line of tramroad, turn left into the road when you meet it, follow it downhill and turn left again in ¾ mile at a T-junction. This road can also be joined by tracks from the foot of the inclined planes climbed on the outward journey.

A walk westwards along the tram road into what is now the Craig y Cilau nature reserve is well worth while. Shortly after rounding a bend to the left you will reach a display panel about the reserve. showing footpaths and also the location of the Eglwys Faen and Agen Allwedd cave systems, the former open to those with suitable experience and equipment. Continuing onwards, approx. 400 yards after the display panel the path bends to the right, following the line of the escarpment, passing a little 'cove' and, shortly afterwards, a short path leading up on the left to the entrance to Eglwys Faen. A further 250 yards along the tramroad, past a small promontory, will be found a bootworn footpath leading down on the right, waymarked with a yellow arrow on a short post. Take this path, forking right at a junction after about 250 yards, following the yellow arrow. Soon after, as you approach a wall, ignore the yellow waymark arrow pointing to the left (unless you wish to continue on for half a mile to the road, turning right when your reach it) and instead turn sharply right and head eastwards, with the wall on your left. Keep straight on when the wall wall turns briefly left (a stile offers yet another alternative route). The wall soon resumes its roughly easterly alignment and the way continues ahead, parallel with and a little way away from the wall (in parts just a wire fence), with Nant Onnau on the other side. Continue until in about half a mile you reach a 'Daren y Cilau Nature Reserve' sign (facing away from you). 50 yards after this the stream flows under the wall from the far side to the path side. After a further 25 yards take a narrow track leading uphill and slightly to the right. Continue on this for approx. ½ mile. Turn left into the road when you meet it, follow it downhill and turn left again in ½ mile at a T-junction.

WALK 5: BRINORE TRAMROAD TO TALYBONT RESERVOIR
Fairly easy walking, initially along the gradually rising tramroad track. There are fine views towards the reservoir and dam.
Starting Point: The towpath at Bridge 143   **Time**: 1½ to 2 hours
Distance: 3½miles   **Height climbed**: 450ft/140m

Cross over bridge 143, heading south. After 50 yards take the waymarked track straight ahead (i.e. ignore the gateway to Dan yr Wenallt on the left) and turn left across the bridge over the old Brecon & Merthyr Railway. Then turn immediately right into the track of the tramroad. (Look briefly behind you to see where the tramway used to run on its way to the wharf at the lime kilns between bridges 142 and 143.)

As you continue ahead, the conifer-clad hillside of Wenallt lies on the left. To the right, just a field away, is the track of the former railway, with Afon Caerfanell beyond and Talybont Forest rising on the far hillside.

In approx. 1 mile, ignore a new Forestry Commission track crossing the tramroad at an angle, leading down to right (but note the junction for your return journey) and continue straight on, signposted Trevil and Brinore Tramroad. Views of the reservoir and dam appear and grow, with splendid displays of rhododendrons by the spillway in early summer.

When apparently abreast of the spillway you pass between ruins to right and left, reputedly the remains of a beer house, and in a further 200 yards come to a gateway, just after a footpath sign to the left leading back and uphill (which provides a route to the canal at bridge 138). Immediately through the gateway turn right over the stile and take the path leading downhill.

After 40 yards, follow the path right and left across a stream gully and continue downhill along the left hand edge of the field, following the bank of the gully. In 100 yards, shortly after an old oak tree, join a wider track leading down to the right. Follow this until you pass through a waymarked gate reach the trackbed of the old railway – now part of the Taff Trail for walkers. Turn left along the track for about 100 yards to reach the dam.

To return to the canal you can cross the dam, turn right and follow the road back via the village of Aber to the drawbridge at Talybont. Alternatively, do NOT cross the dam but retreat and turn left (north) back in to the Taff Trail. Follow the trackbed towards Talybont until, after about ¼ mile, the way ahead is prohibited. Bear right up the Forestry Commission track, signposted Taff Trail, and turn left back into the Brinore Tramway for Talybont.

WELSH GLOSSARY

It can add interest to your holiday to be able to understand Welsh place names on the map and on signs around you. The following list should enable you to make an intelligent guess at the meaning of some of the bridge, mountain and other place names along the canal. These are often very local in their significance. Many of the bridges are accommodation bridges, connecting together parts of an estate divided by the canal, and may take their name from the property they serve. As in English, words are often combined, as for example in 'Troed-y-rhiw' – foot of the hill. Sometimes, English influence has corrupted the spelling, as for example in Govilon (Gefailon) and Panteague (Panteg).

Note that in Welsh the initial letters of feminine nouns beginning with the letters b,c,d,g,m,p or t change when following the definite article. Qualifying adjectives also 'mutate'. Sometimes, the mutated form will be found without the definite article, lost through usage. Where two spellings are given in the glossary, separated by a comma, the second is the mutated form. Plurals have generally been omitted, except where likely to be encountered along the canal.

Although the part of Wales through which the canal runs is predominantly English-speaking, Welsh is still spoken amongst hill farmers around Brecon. It can occasionally be heard spoken in Brecon itself.

aber – river mouth or confluence (as in Aberhonddu, the Welsh name for Brecon, where the Honddu flows into the Usk)
afon – river
allt – hillside, wood, wooded hillside
arglwydd – lord
bach, fach – little, small
beili – enclosure
blaen – head (of valley), source, end
brân, frân pl.**brain** – crow
bryn – hill
bwlch – gap, pass
cae – field (closed)
caer, gaer – fort
calch – lime
camlas, gamlas – canal
capel – chapel

carn, garn – cairn, heap, prominence
carreg, garreg – rock, stone
cerrig, gerrig – rocks, stones
castell – castle
cefn – ridge, back
celli, gelli – grove, copse
celyn, gelyn – holly
cil, gil – nook, corner, recess
coch, goch – red
coed, goed – trees, wood
craig, graig – rock, crag
cribyn – crest
croes, groes – cross, crossroads
crug, grug – mound, knoll, cairn
cwm – valley, depression
cythraul – demon
dan – below, under
darren – rocky slope, rock face, precipice

derwen, dderwen pl.derw – oak
du, ddu – black
dwfn – deep
dŵr – water
dyffryn – valley
eirin – plums
eithinog – place of gorse
eglwys – church
esgair – ridge
fan – peak
ffawyddog – place of beech trees
ffynnon – well, spring, fountain
garth – headland, enclosure
gefail, efail – smithy, forge
glan, lan – bank
glas, las – blue, green
goytre – home in wood (coed–tre)
gwern, wern – marsh, alder grove
gwyn (gwen), wen – white, fair
gwyrdd – green
hafod – summer dwelling
hendre – winter dwelling
heol – road
hwyaid – ducks
isaf – lower, lowest
llan – church (originally sacred enclosure)
    usually followed by name
    of saint, e.g.:

Llanddetty –	church of	St. Detwys
Llanellen	"	St.Helen
Llanelli	"	St. Elli
Llanfeigan	"	St. Meugan
Llanfoist	"	St. Ffwyst
Llanfrynach	"	St. Brynach
Llangattock	"	St. Catwg
Llangynidr	"	St. Cynidr

llech – slab, slate, flat stone
llwybr – path
llwyd – grey, brown
llwyn – bush, grove
llyn – lake, pool

llys – court, hall
maen – stone
maes – open field, plain
mawr, fawr – big
march, pl.meirch – horse
melin, felin – mill
moel, foel – bare (hilltop or hill)
miarth – enclosure
mynydd – mountain
nant – brook, stream
neuadd – hall
newydd – new
ochr – side
pandy – fulling mill
pant – hollow, valley
parc – park, parkland
pedwar, pedair – four
pen – head, end, top
pentre – village
pistyll – well, spring, waterfall
poeth – hot
pont, bont – bridge
porth – gateway, porch, entrance
pwll – pit, pool
rhiw – hill, hillside, slope (track up)
rhyd – ford
tal – end, front, head
teg – fair
tir – land
tor – break (of slope)
tre (tref), dre (dref) – home, village,
               town
troed – foot
twmpath – hillock
twyn – mound, hillock, knoll
ty – house
uchaf – upper, higher, highest
y, yr , 'r – the (of the)
yn – in
ynys – island
ysgol – school
ystrad – valley bottom

69

BRIDGE & DISTANCE TABLE

Br. No.	Miles from Pontymoile		Miles from Brecon
52	0.00	Pontymoile Bridge	33.35
	0.13	Aqueduct	33.22
53	0.27	Pontypool Road Bridge	33.08
54	0.62	Cabbage Bridge (dem'd)	32.73
55	0.80	Jockey Bridge	32.55
	0.82	Winding Point	32.53
56	0.94	Squires Bridge	32.41
		(or Ty-poeth Br.)	
	0.98	Winding Point	32.37
	1.63	Winding Point	31.72
57	1.66	Lower Wern Bridge	31.69
58	1.83	Upper Wern Bridge	31.52
59	2.15	Keepers Bridge	31.20
60	2.28	Govera Bridge	31.07
61	2.46	Troed-y-rhiw Bridge	30.89
62	2.76	High Bridge	30.59
	2.86	Winding Point	30.49
63	3.15	Mamhilad Bridge	30.20
64	3.33	Skinners Bridge	30.02
65	3.46	Mortimers Bridge	29.89
66	3.64	Brook Farm Bridge	29.71
67	3.86	Pentre Bridge	29.49
68	4.05	Croes-y-pant Bridge	29.30
69	4.28	High House Bridge	29.07
70	4.46	Birdspool Bridge	28.89
	4.54	Winding Point	28.81
71	4.90	Parc-y-brain Lower Br.	28.45
72	4.98	Parc-y-brain Upper Br.	28.37
73	5.24	Penrheol Bridge	28.11
	5.40	Winding Point	27.95
74	5.44	Saron Bridge	27.91
	5.76	Winding Point	27.59
	5.83	Goytre Wharf	27.52
75	6.04	Jenkin Rosser's Bridge	27.31
	6.09	Winding Point	27.26
76	6.37	Lapstone Bridge	26.98
77	6.46	Preacher's Bridge	26.89
		(or Cottage Br.)	
78	6.83	Mill Turn Bridge	26.52
	6.9	Mill Turn	26.5
	7.15	Winding Point	26.20
79	7.21	Mount Pleasant Lower Br.	26.14
80	7.38	Mount Pleasant Upper Br.	25.97
81	7.53	Llanover Bridge	25.82
82	7.65	Pwllyrhwyaid Bridge	25.70
83	7.91	Beech Tree Bridge	25.44
84	8.12	Ty-coch Bridge	25.23
85	8.27	Thimbles Bridge	25.08
	8.5	Ochram Turn	24.9
86	8.70	Ochram Turn Bridge	24.65
		(or Cwm-celyn Br.)	
87	8.84	Poplar Bridge	24.51
	8.91	Winding Point	24.44
88	9.00	Twyn-glas Bridge	24.35
		(or Roberts Br.)	
89	9.09	Barn Bridge	24.26
90	9.42	Morgans Bridge	23.93
91	9.56	Wooden Bridge	23.79
		(or Llanellen Br.)	
92	9.83	Heol-gerrig Bridge	23.52
	10.15	Winding Point	23.20
93	10.22	Richards Farm Bridge	23.13
	10.4	Castle Turn	23.0
94	10.65	Castle Lower Bridge	22.70
95	10.84	Castle Upper Bridge	22.51
	11.43	Tods Bridge	21.92
	11.44	Winding Point	21.91
	11.92	White House Turn	21.43
96	12.31	Govilon Quarry Bridge	21.04
		(or Lower Turn Br.)	
97	12.54	Govilon Yard Bridge	20.81
	12.59	Winding Point	20.76
	12.74	Railway Bridge	20.61
98	12.91	Govilon Stn. Rd. Bridge	20.44
	13.04	Aqueduct	20.31
	13.06	Govilon Dry Dock	20.29
	13.17	Road aqueduct	20.18
99	13.34	Llanwenarth Bridge	20.01
100	13.45	Humphreys Bridge (ex DB)	19.90
101	13.76	Heol-yr-Allt Bridge	19.59
	13.85	Winding Point	19.50
	13.95	Heads of the Valleys Br.	19.40
102	13.98	Ty-gwyn Bridge	19.37
103	14.50	Gilwern Bridge	18.85
	14.64	Aqueduct	18.71
	14.67	Gilwern Basin	18.68
104	14.76	Auckland Bridge	18.59
	14.97	Winding Point	18.38
105	15.03	Sand Bridge	18.32
106	15.32	Ffynnon-yr-eirin Bridge	18.03
107	15.67	Dan-y-graig Bridge	17.68
	15.72	Winding Point	17.63
108	16.13	Craig-yr-allt-llwyd Bridge	17.22
109	16.58	Dan-y-Parc Bridge	16.77
		(or Dark Br.)	
	16.67	Windy Corner	16.68
	16.72	Winding Point	16.63
110	16.86	Pen-pedair-heol Bridge	16.49

No.	Dist.	Feature	Dist.		No.	Dist.	Feature	Dist.
111	17.01	Wooden Bridge	16.34			24.76	Snake Bridge	8.59
112	17.20	Park Bridge	16.15		140	24.89	Lower Wenallt Bridge	8.46
		(or Pont-y-Parc)			141	25.09	Upper Wenallt Bridge	8.26
113	17.42	Llwmws Bridge	15.93			25.4	Ashford Tunnel	8.0
		(or Pont Twyn-cythraul)			142	26.05	Graig-las Bridge	7.30
114	17.82	Lower Yard Bridge	15.53			26.09	Winding point	7.26
115	17.90	Upper Yard Bridge	15.45			26.21	Railway Bridge	7.14
	18.01	Winding Point	15.34		143	26.23	White Hart Bridge	7.12
116	18.29	Ffawyddog Bridge	15.06			26.28	Aqueduct	7.07
		(or Pont Llangatwg)			144	26.44	Talybont Drawbridge	6.91
117	18.39	Dan-y-garth Bridge	14.96		145	26.61	Benaiah Bridge	6.74
118	18.68	Union Bridge	14.67				(or Almshouses Br.)	
		(or Workhouse Br.)			146	26.76	Gilston Bridge	6.59
119	18.95	Folly Bridge	14.40		147	27.19	Cross Oak Bridge	6.16
120	19.49	Baylis Bridge	13.86		148	27.38	Cross Oak Drawbridge	5.97
121	19.67	Llwyncelyn Bridge	13.68		149	27.50	Gethinog Drawbridge	5.85
	19.88	Glan Usk Bridge	13.47		150	27.63	Penawr Drawbridge	5.72
122	20.18	Fro Bridge	13.17		151	27.79	Penawr Bridge	5.56
123	20.43	Pen-y-bryn Bridge	12.92		152	28.30	Castle Bridge	5.05
124	20.59	Spiteful Inn Bridge	12.76		153	28.50	Cross Keys Bridge	4.85
125	20.88	Dyfnant Bridge	12.47		154	28.61	Pencelli Bridge	4.74
126	21.26	Aber-hoywe Bridge	12.09			28.64	Winding Point & Slip.	4.71
	21.36	Winding Point	11.99		155	28.70	Pencelli Court Drawbr.	4.65
127	21.52	Old House Bridge	11.83		156	29.01	Low Bridge	4.34
128	21.74	Panteague Drawbr. (ex)	11.61		157	29.43	Llan-brynean Bridge	3.92
	21.81	Winding Point	11.54			29.66	Menascin Aqueduct	3.69
129	21.96	Panteague Bridge	11.39		158	29.84	Storehouse Bridge	3.51
130	22.21	Aber-yail Bridge	11.14		159	29.97	Ty-newydd No.1 Bridge	3.38
	22.59	Winding Point	10.76			30.01	Cambrian Cruisers Marina	3.34
131	22.61	Yard Bridge	10.74		160	30.15	Ty-newydd No.2 Bridge	3.20
132	22.92	Lower Lock Bridge	10.43		161	30.74	Bell Ear Bridge	2.61
L64	22.93	Lower Lock	10.42			30.95	Winding Point	2.40
133	23.03	Coach and Horses Br.	10.32		162	30.98	Turn Bridge	2.37
	23.14	Winding Point	10.21			31.07	Brynich Aqueduct	2.28
	23.15	Aqueduct	10.20		163	31.21	Cefn Brynich Bridge	2.14
L65	23.20	Coombes/Depot Lock	10.15		L69	31.22	Brynich Lock	2.13
134	23.24	Coombes Lock Bridge	10.11		164	31.88	Brynich Bridge	1.47
L66	23.50	Gwlawcoed Lock	9.85			32.07	A40 Bridge	1.28
L67	23.54	Little Lock	9.81		165	32.98	Watton Bridge	0.37
L68	23.56	Top Lock	9.79			33.04	Winding Point	0.31
135	23.65	Top Lock Bridge	9.70		166	33.25	Gas Works Bridge	0.10
136	23.84	Workhouse Bridge	9.51				Probert Basin	
137	24.04	Dan-y-graig Bridge	9.31		167	33.31	Dadford Bridge	0.04
138	24.33	Parsons Bridge	9.02				Theatre Basin	
139	24.68	Llanddetty Bridge	8.67			33.35	End (present)	0.00

Distance figures are based on careful measurements from 1:25000 OS maps and are estimated to the second decimal place to allow close determination of distances between adjacent features. The overall total is approx. 0.1 mile greater than 'official' figures. Checks with a waywiser over 20% of the canal, taping of four quarter-mile sections and comparison with a GWR profile of c.1881 suggest possible inaccuracies in past official sources and milepost positions.

MONMOUTHSHIRE CANAL

Pontymoile to Five Locks, Cwmbran

For forty years, navigation below Pontymoile was impeded by the culverted
channel through Crown Bridge, No. 48.
The rebuilding of the bridge in 1994 by
Torfaen Borough Council was the first
significant progress in the eventual
restoration of the Monmouthshire canal,
allowing boats once more to travel as far
south as Five Locks on the outskirts of
Cwmbran, albeit with some difficulty. In
1996 a new basin was constructed by
British Waterways at Five Locks. Grants
from the EEC, the Welsh Development
Agency and Gwent C.C. helped to make
all this possible.

Really effective dredging in 2003 has
restored the depth of water and cruising
to Five Locks is much to be encouraged.
It will help to keep the channel open and
demonstrate interest among boaters and
local people in the aim of eventual
restoration to Newport.

GRIFFITHSTOWN

SHOPS AND SERVICES: (50/49)
Good range of local shops and services
in Windsor Road, including butcher, baker,
grocer, chemist, newsagent, pet food, hairdresser, post office and bank (Lloyds

PUBLIC HOUSES:
Masons Arms [boaters book] (50)
Open Hearth [boaters book] (49)

HEALTH CENTRE: (49)

SEBASTOPOL

CROWN BRIDGE (48)
The Crown,
Post office, telephone, fish & chicken
bar, hair stylist, wine stores.

CWMBRAN

FIVE LOCKS (45)
Cross Keys Inn [Boaters book].
General stores
PONTNEWYDD (44)
Old Bridge End Inn

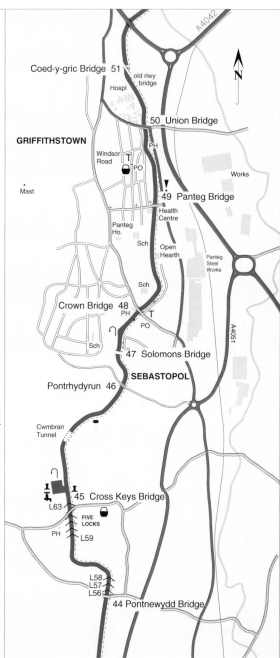

Note: As most boats will enter this section of canal via Pontymoile, the narrative assumes a direction of travel southwards towards Newport.

Once through bridge 52 and the new A472 bridge, the canal passes a playing field on the left, with intermittent views across the field to the distant gas works and the rather nearer factory. To the right, trees line the canal.

Bridge 51 is followed so closely by the skew railway bridge that the path leading uphill from the bridge passes through an arch in the masonry of the railway bridge. Downstream, trees on the right soon thin out to give views of the approaching hospital complex, which occupies much of the offside until the next bridge. On the left is the tree-lined railway embankment. About 200yds before the next bridge note the concrete blocks that stand on each side of the canal. These once supported a bridge for a narrow-gauge railway carrying coal to the hospital.

Bridge 50, flat, low and rebuilt, is a convenient point to leave for the shops in Windsor Road – cross the bridge and turn left by a general stores and off licence and continue along Broad Street to Windsor Road. To return to the canal continue along Oxford Street and at the end turn left to rejoin the canal at bridge 49.

Between bridges 50 and 49, the canal passes the towpath entrance and beer garden of the Masons Arms before winding through a sinuous bend with street views on the right. Houses now back on to the towpath, some so low that first floor window sills seem at towpath eye level. Approaching bridge 49, longer gardens on the offside come down to the water's edge. Some owners clearly appreciate their waterside location and an interesting piece of topiary work suggests that the Welshman's home, like the Englishman's, is his castle. The variegated sandstone end wall of Griffithstown Baptist Church follows, the various commemorative stones placed during construction interestingly facing the canal.

Bridge 49, flat, rebuilt and without a towpath is very low, offering an 'air draft' of barely six feet. Once through the bridge the canal resumes a more rural aspect as the Panteg Health Centre gives way gradually to playing fields and schools. To the left are glimpses of the approaching Panteg Works of Avesta Polarit, one of British Waterways' customers for water.

200yds downstream of the bridge stands the Open Hearth, once called the Railway Inn. The Open Hearth is noted for its food and large range of real ales. Reaching here was the pinnacle of navigational achievement, particularly for large boats, during the many years when the canal was barely navigable below Pontymoile. A boaters' book is still kept to record those who arrive by water. While signing, you can read of the struggles of those who have gone before.

From the Open Hearth to Crown Bridge, No. 48, houses line the back of the towpath, among them Panteg Nursing Home – note the stained glass kingfisher panel in the door. At the rebuilt Crown Bridge, the pub of that name is accompanied by a post office, a telephone, a wine stores and a fish and chicken bar. 200yds after the bridge is a new winding point.

The canal soon leaves Sebastopol behind and, after a tree-lined stretch downstream of bridge 47, enters open country with views of distant hills and the rather nearer works of Owens Corning. Bridge 46, flat, low and concrete, is followed by slow bends right and left on the approach to the 87yd long Cwmbran Tunnel. Housing returns soon after the tunnel and lines much of the offside on the approach to the new canal basin and Cross Keys Bridge at 'Five Locks'. There is a useful general stores in Five Locks Road.

A ten minute walk south along the towpath will take you past locks 58 to 56, with their concreted top gates, and then by a water-lilied stretch to the landscaped locks at the Old Bridge End Inn.

BRIDGE & DISTANCE TABLE

Br. No.	Miles below Pontymoile	
52		Pontymoile Bridge
51	0.20	Coed-y-gric Bridge
	0.21	Railway Bridge (disused)
50	0.48	Union Bridge
49	0.81	Panteg (or Kemys) Bridge
48	1.27	Crown Bridge
	1.40	Winding Point
47	1.47	Solomons Bridge
46	1.63	Pontrhydyrun
	2.0	Cwmbran Tunnel
45	2.29	Cross Keys Bridge
		Five Locks

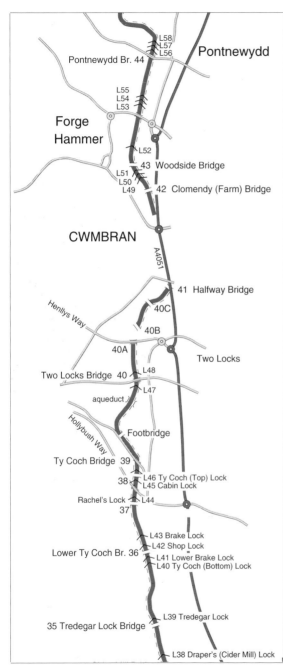

Pontnewydd Br. 44

L58
L57
L56

Pontnewydd

L55
L54
L53

Forge Hammer

L52

43 Woodside Bridge

L51
L50
L49   42 Clomendy (Farm) Bridge

CWMBRAN

A4051

41 Halfway Bridge

40C

40B

40A

Henllys Way

Two Locks

Two Locks Bridge 40   L48

L47

aqueduct

Hollybush Way

Footbridge

Ty Coch Bridge 39

38   L46 Ty Coch (Top) Lock
      L45 Cabin Lock

Rachel's Lock   L44
37

L43 Brake Lock
L42 Shop Lock
Lower Ty Coch Br. 36   L41 Lower Brake Lock
                        L40 Ty Coch (Bottom) Lock

L39 Tredegar Lock

35 Tredegar Lock Bridge

L38 Draper's (Cider Mill) Lock

South of bridges 44, old and new, the canal continues. Locks and side pounds survive in various stages of preservation, decay and infill. At times the canal disappears briefly but the line is easy to follow and the walking pleasant.

A lock cottage survives by the ruins of lock 52, followed on the left by the New Bridgend Inn. Once past the remains of locks 51 to 49, the canal begins to lose its semi-rural look as it enters Cwmbran Retail Park. 'Crazy paving' bridges cross the canal just before the channel ends. Follow the path as it leaves the canal to run beside the A4051. Cross Greenforge Way (care required) and take the slope leading upwards on the far side. Fork left shortly before the top and follow the path to rejoin the canal in Star Street, the water having been piped under Greenforge Way. An imaginative aqueduct and back pumping scheme is planned to replace the missing section.

The canal now passes through the suburbs of Cwmbran, the numerous culverted road crossings representing further obstacles to be overcome before navigation can be restored. Despite the housing, nesting swans may be found along this section in springtime. Approaching Henllys Way, there is a short break in the channel where it is overlaid by Bellevue Road.

Two Locks Road separates the now cascaded locks that give it and the neighbourhood their name. The Ebenezer Baptist chapel is prominent on the right.

Below lock 47 the channel narrows and a rebuilt aqueduct takes the canal across a stream. At bridge 39 the towpath changes sides. Concrete fishing stagings will be seen at regular intervals from now on.

Immediately after lock 45 the canal passes beneath the new Hollybush Way, the towpath using a separate tunnel.

Cwmbran is now left behind as the canal enters a delightful three mile rural stretch to the outskirts of Malpas. The long disused locks in the Ty Coch flight quietly await the restorer's hand.

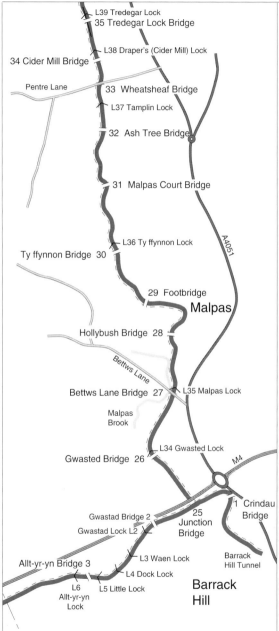

L39 Tredegar Lock
35 Tredegar Lock Bridge

L38 Draper's (Cider Mill) Lock

34 Cider Mill Bridge

Pentre Lane

33 Wheatsheaf Bridge

L37 Tamplin Lock

32 Ash Tree Bridge

31 Malpas Court Bridge

L36 Ty ffynnon Lock

A4051

Ty ffynnon Bridge 30

29 Footbridge

Malpas

Hollybush Bridge 28

Bettws Lane

Bettws Lane Bridge 27   L35 Malpas Lock

Malpas
Brook

L34 Gwasted Lock

Gwasted Bridge 26

M4

1 Crindau
Bridge

Gwastad Bridge 2   25
Junction
Gwastad Lock L2   Bridge

Barrack
Hill Tunnel

Allt-yr-yn Bridge 3   L3 Waen Lock

L4 Dock Lock

L6   L5 Little Lock   Barrack
Allt-yr-yn   Hill
Lock

Away to the left can be seen a distant water tower before the canal reaches Tredegar and Draper's Locks, the latter by the derelict buildings of Cider Mill Farm.

Soon after Pentre Lane has briefly intruded into the rural scene, the canal reaches Tamplins Lock, the first of a series of four now fully restored. After Ash Tree Bridge a pleasant wood appears on the left, speckled white with wood anemones in the spring.

Signs of civilisation begin to appear on the approach to Malpas Court Bridge, with distant houses and flats on the outskirts of Malpas on the left. Soon keen ears will notice the distant hum of the M4. Ty ffynnon lock, like others on the canal, has the bywash emerging in the side wall below the lock, a typical Dadford feature.

Rounding the bend before Hollybush Bridge there is housing on the left with gardens reaching down to the waters edge, their moorings waiting expectantly. To the right there are still fields, and now a sports ground, with Bettws beyond. The Malpas Brook approaches the canal before turning at a guillotine sluice to run roughly alongside. Restoration plans include the use of a canalised Malpas Brook to link the canal from near Barrack Hill to the River Usk.

The restored Malpas Lock soon follows, the top gate hinged, like Tamplin Lock, to avoid obstructing the towpath. Bettws Lane crosses immediately after the lock. There is a small slip way soon after the bridge. At Gwasted Lock, the towpath crosses over the bridge to the east side. The section of canal from here to the present end of the canal at Barrack Hill tunnel is navigable and was used for the National Trail Boat Rally in 2000, which helped to raise public interest in the canal.

Beyond the motorway lies the junction with the Crumlin arm. A 'totem pole' marks the spot, one of a thousand erected by the Royal Bank of Scotland to mark the creation of the national cycle network. It is worth taking the brief walk to the left, along the main line of the canal through Crindau Bridge, to the mouth of

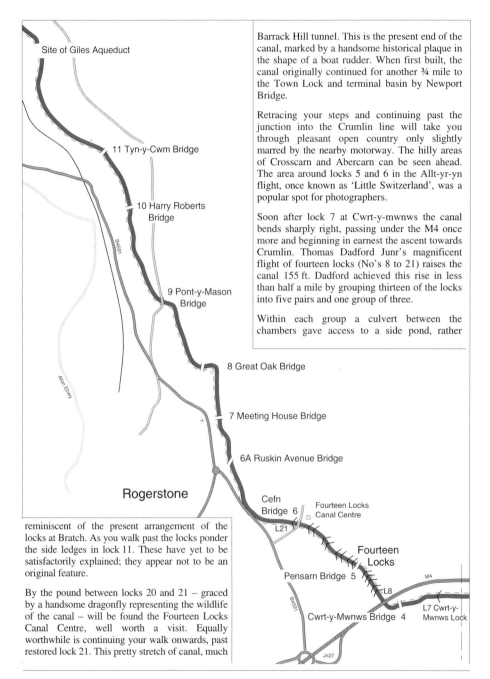

Barrack Hill tunnel. This is the present end of the canal, marked by a handsome historical plaque in the shape of a boat rudder. When first built, the canal originally continued for another ¾ mile to the Town Lock and terminal basin by Newport Bridge.

Retracing your steps and continuing past the junction into the Crumlin line will take you through pleasant open country only slightly marred by the nearby motorway. The hilly areas of Crosscarn and Abercarn can be seen ahead. The area around locks 5 and 6 in the Allt-yr-yn flight, once known as 'Little Switzerland', was a popular spot for photographers.

Soon after lock 7 at Cwrt-y-mwnws the canal bends sharply right, passing under the M4 once more and beginning in earnest the ascent towards Crumlin. Thomas Dadford Junr's magnificent flight of fourteen locks (No's 8 to 21) raises the canal 155 ft. Dadford achieved this rise in less than half a mile by grouping thirteen of the locks into five pairs and one group of three.

Within each group a culvert between the chambers gave access to a side pond, rather

reminiscent of the present arrangement of the locks at Bratch. As you walk past the locks ponder the side ledges in lock 11. These have yet to be satisfactorily explained; they appear not to be an original feature.

By the pound between locks 20 and 21 – graced by a handsome dragonfly representing the wildlife of the canal – will be found the Fourteen Locks Canal Centre, well worth a visit. Equally worthwhile is continuing your walk onwards, past restored lock 21. This pretty stretch of canal, much

Map labels:
Site of Giles Aqueduct
11 Tyn-y-Cwm Bridge
10 Harry Roberts Bridge
9 Pont-y-Mason Bridge
8 Great Oak Bridge
7 Meeting House Bridge
6A Ruskin Avenue Bridge
Rogerstone
Cefn Bridge 6
Fourteen Locks Canal Centre
L21
Fourteen Locks
Pensarn Bridge 5
L8
Cwrt-y-Mwnws Bridge 4
L7 Cwrt-y-Mwnws Lock
M4
Jn27
B4591
Afon Ebwy

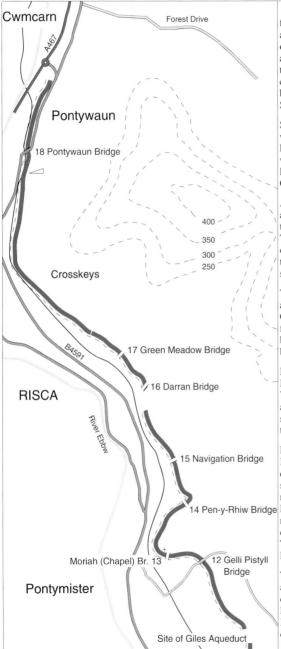

Cwmcarn

Forest Drive

A467

Pontywaun

18 Pontywaun Bridge

400
350
300
250

Crosskeys

17 Green Meadow Bridge

B4591

16 Darran Bridge

RISCA

River Ebbw

15 Navigation Bridge

14 Pen-y-Rhiw Bridge

Moriah (Chapel) Br. 13

12 Gelli Pistyll Bridge

Pontymister

Site of Giles Aqueduct

favoured by moorhens, follows the contour all the way to Cwmcarn, with rising ground on the right. To the left the ground falls away down to the Ebbw valley with views to the hills beyond. Housing on the right continues for some way; on the left a road briefly approaches, bringing the Rising Sun within convenient reach.

Soon after the pretty Meeting House Bridge, with the Bethesda Chapel visible on the left, the canal bends sharply to the left with Culvert Cottage nestling in the bend. Fields open up on the right after Great Oak Bridge as the housing is left behind.

A break in the trees lining the towpath after Pont y Mason Bridge gives a brief tree-framed view down the drive of Oak Tree Cottage to the valley below. Views open up ahead, and intermittently between trees on the left over the site of Roger-stone power station to the hills beyond.

The 5¼ MCCo mile post survives soon after Tyn y Cwm Bridge. The site of the Giles aqueduct, demolished in 1973, soon follows. Known locally as the 'leaky bridge' it was a cause of icing on the road below.

Nestling in the bank 100yds after the Moriah Chapel Bridge lies the Prince of Wales, a convenient resting point for admiring the lovely view ahead. There is soon an equally fine view to the hills on the left.

Piled offside edging after Navigation Bridge supports the road to the Darren quarry, visible through the firs. The road soon 'takes over' the canal, which is rejoined after crossing Darran Bridge. From here to the end the canal is navigable and the pleasant countryside continues with fine views on both sides. The trip boat Jemima Morris is based at Pontywaun.

The end of the canal is reached ¼ mile after Pontywaun Bridge. Originally it continued for another 3 miles through 12 locks to Crumlin, where it met the Beaufort Tramroad bringing coal and iron down from the Beaufort Ironworks.

BIBLIOGRAPHY

Brecknock & Abergavenny and Monmouth-   R. Alan Stevens, Goose & Son, 1974
shire Canals. Towpath Guide No.2
The Canals of South Wales and the Border   Charles Hadfield, David & Charles, 1967
The Brecon and Abergavenny Canal   Deb, Jill and Howard Jones, 1983 edit.
Cruising along the Mon & Brec Canal   James Eyles, The Starling Press, 1980
The Clydach Gorge   John van Laun, 3rd edit.1989,
    Brecon Beacons National Park Committee.

Rape of the Fair Country   A. Cordell, Victor Gollanz 1959, Coronet 1976
Cordell Country   Chris Barber, Blorenge Books, 1985
Here and There on the Monmouthshire,   Ken Haynes, Printed by The Starling Press, 1988
Brecon & Abergavenny Canal
An Introduction to the History   Dorothea Watkins,
of Llangynidr   Llangynidr Local History Society, 1986
The Talybont Saga   David Tipper, Dwr Cymru Welsh Water, 1993

FURTHER READING:

Tramroads of the Brecknock &   Gordon Rattenbury,
Abergavenny Canal   Railway and Canal Historical Society, 1980
Early Limestone Railways   John van Laun, The Newcomen Society 2001
The Hay and Kington Railways   Gordon Rattenbury & Ray Cook, RCHS, 1996
The Seven Hills of Abergavenny   Chris Barber, Blorenge Books, 1992
The Llangattock Escarpment   Kevin Walker, Heritage Guides, 1985
Guide to Table Mountain   Kevin Walker, Heritage Guides, 1986

USEFUL LEAFLETS:

Monmouthshire and Brecon Canal;   Gwent Trust for Nature Conservation,
a Guide to its Natural History   (awaiting reprinting)
Abergavenny Town Trail   Abergavenny Civic Society
A Walk Around Abergavenny   Gwyn Jones, Abergavenny Local Hist. Society
Three Walks from Govilon   Information Sheet No.27,
    Brecon Beacons National Park Commitee

Discover the Clydach Gorge   Blaenau Gwent B.C (currently out of print)
Discover Gilwern   Blaenau Gwent B.C. (currently out of print)
A Look at Crickhowell   Brecon Beacons National Park Committee
Talybont Valley   Brecon Beacons National Park Committee
A Look at Brecon   Brecon Beacons National Park Committee
The Hay Tramway   Planning Information Service,
    Powys County Council

PRIMARY SOURCE MATERIAL:

B &A Canal Co. Minute Books etc.   Public Record Office, Kew,
    Refs: RAIL812, Pieces 1 to 15
The Maybery Papers   National Library of Wales
The Fowler Papers   Powys County Archives Office